D0040398

CHARLES SPURGEON
❧ *Christian Living Classics* ❧

A Passion for Holiness in a Believer's Life

❧ Compiled and Edited by ROBERT HALL ❧

Emerald Books
P.O. Box 635 • Lynnwood, Washington 98046

CHARLES SPURGEON
CHRISTIAN LIVING CLASSICS

Grace Abounding in a Believer's Life

A Passion for Holiness in a Believer's Life

The Power of Prayer in a Believer's Life

Spiritual Warfare in a Believer's Life

The Triumph of Faith in a Believer's Life

What the Holy Spirit Does in a Believer's Life

SPURGEON

A Passion for Holiness in a Believer's Life

CHRISTIAN LIVING CLASSICS

Emerald Books are distributed by YWAM Publishing. For a full list of titles, including other classics, call 1-800-922-2143 or visit our website at www.ywampublishing.com.

Published by Emerald Books
P.O. Box 635
Lynnwood, Washington 98046

Scripture quotations are taken from the King James Version of the Bible.

ISBN 1-883002-07-9

Printed in the United States of America.

To

Nils and Gloria Strom

"Without having seen him
you love him;
though you do not now see him
you believe in him and rejoice
with unutterable and exalted joy."

About the Editor

ROBERT HALL is the pseudonym for Lance Wubbels, the managing editor of Bethany House Publishers. His interest in the writings of Charles Spurgeon began while doing research on an editorial project that required extensive reading of Spurgeon's sermons. He discovered a wealth of sermon classics that are filled with practical, biblical insight for every believer and written in a timeless manner that makes them as relevant today as the day they were spoken. His desire is to select and present Spurgeon's writings in a way that will appeal to a wide audience of readers and allow one of the greatest preachers of all time to enrich believers' lives.

About the Author

CHARLES HADDON SPURGEON (1834–1892) was the remarkable British "Boy Preacher of the Fens" who became one of the truly greatest preachers of all time. Coming from a flourishing country pastorate in 1854, he accepted a call to pastor London's New Park Street Chapel. This building soon proved too small and so work on Spurgeon's Metropolitan Tabernacle was begun in 1859. Meanwhile his weekly sermons were being printed and having a remarkable sale—25,000 copies every week in 1865 and translated into more than twenty languages.

Spurgeon built the Metropolitan Tabernacle into a congregation of over 6,000 and added well over 14,000 members during his thirty-eight-year London ministry. The combination of his clear voice, his mastery of language, his sure grasp of Scripture, and a deep love for Christ produced some of the noblest preaching of any age. An astounding 3,561 sermons have been preserved in sixty-three volumes, *The New Park Street Pulpit* and *The Metropolitan Tabernacle Pulpit*, from which the chapters of this book have been selected and edited.

During his lifetime, Spurgeon is estimated to have preached to 10,000,000 people. He remains history's most widely read preacher. There is more available material written by Spurgeon than by any other Christian author, living or dead. His sixty-three volumes of sermons stand as the largest set of books by a single author in the history of Christianity, comprising the equivalent to the twenty-seven volumes of the ninth edition of the *Encyclopedia Britannica*.

Contents

Introduction 11
1. Believers Free from the Power of Sin 15
2. A Passion for Holiness 31
3. Perfecting Holiness 45
4. Crucified with Christ 57
5. The Hope That Purifies 73
6. Death for Sin, and Death to Sin 87
7. Holiness, the Law of God's House 103
8. Three Crosses 119
9. Holy Longings 135
10. The Sixth Beatitude 148
11. A Holy Resolve 165
12. The Holy Road 176

Introduction

"WHEN OUR LIVES COME to be written at last," Charles Spurgeon once wrote, "God grant that they be not only our *sayings* but our *sayings* and *doings*." A fair assessment of Spurgeon's remarkable life and ministry must include both.

Considered by his peers then and now as "one of evangelical Christianity's immortals," Charles Spurgeon preached his first sermon in 1850 at the age of sixteen. He astonished his listeners with his oratorical powers, and from then on he was in constant demand as a speaker. The "boy preacher" from Essex, as he was called in his early years, would go on to nearly four decades of ministry in London and built the Metropolitan Tabernacle into the world's largest independent congregration during the nineteenth century. Davenport Northrop, a contemporary of Spurgeon, called him "the most celebrated preacher of modern times . . . the most conspicuous figure in the religious world . . . the Saul among the prophets, standing head and shoulder above the others."

No building in London seemed big enough to house all those who wanted to hear him preach. There is no doubt that the Spirit of God launched a new era of ministry that exploded in England's capital city, and the shock waves of that explosion can still be felt today. Why was that so? What was it that shaped the life of Charles Spurgeon that so drew people to the gospel of Jesus Christ?

Lewis Drummond has written a fascinating description of Spurgeon's life in the introduction to his recent biography, *Spurgeon: Prince of Preachers*. Drummond says:

Above all, God's man, to be significantly used by God, must be just that: *God's Man*. Spurgeon had many unusual gifts. He was a man with a brilliant mind and a captivating personality. He possessed a marvelous voice and his natural gift of oratory skills amazed the multitudes that came to hear him. He could organize work brilliantly. But primarily, he loved Jesus Christ with all his heart. He was a Christian man in the full biblical sense of the word. Spurgeon's deepest desire centered in living a life of God-honoring Christian holiness. . . .

Simply put, Charles Haddon Spurgeon, lifted up by the reviving and quickening power of the Holy Spirit, began a pilgrimage that would ultimately give England, and the world, one of the greatest pastoral, evangelistic, social ministries ever seen. That opinion is shared by many, not just a few superficially enamored admirers. Spurgeon was a giant in effecting revival.

While Spurgeon did not participate in the holiness movements popular among late nineteenth-century evangelicals, he had a strong doctrine of sanctification and the work of the Holy Spirit in a believer's life. Spurgeon saw sanctification as a vital experience, and he constantly proclaimed the power of the Holy Spirit to regenerate, revive, indwell, and empower the Christian. He declared:

I would sooner be holy than happy if the two things would be divorced. Were it possible for a man always to sorrow and yet to be pure, I would choose the sorrow if I might win the purity, for to be free from the power of sin, to be made to love holiness, is true happiness.

Spurgeon had one consuming purpose and goal: to exalt his Savior in godly living and preach the gospel with power. At the end of his life, Spurgeon's *sayings* and *doings* truly matched up well.

Every believer in Jesus Christ shares the same concern that his life reflect the holiness and purity of the gospel. But in some Christian circles, holiness is distorted with perfectionism. In other circles, holiness is cast aside as an impossibility and irrelevant. Still others promote outward displays of the power of the Holy Spirit but neglect the inner life of the believer. None of these reflect the dynamic, biblical view of sanctification and personal holiness that is available to all Christians.

I invite you to read these twelve select chapters on holiness as you would listen to a trusted and skilled pastor. Nourished by his profound submission to Scripture and Puritan theology, Spurgeon deeply appreciated God's transcendent holiness, the vast gulf separating it from man's sinfulness, and the atonement that spanned that gulf. You will not be disappointed.

Careful editing has helped to sharpen the focus of these sermons while retaining the authentic and timeless flavor they undoubtedly bring.

Sin is a domineering force. No one can sin up to a fixed point and then say to sin, "This is as far as you go." Sin is an imperious power, and where it dwells it is hungry for the mastery. Just as our Lord, when He enters the soul, will never be content with a divided dominion, so is it with sin. Sin labors to bring our entire personality under subjection. Hence, we are compelled to strive daily against this ambitious principle. According to the working of the Spirit of God in us, we wrestle against sin that it may not have dominion over us. Sin has unquestioned dominion over multitudes of human hearts, and in some it has set up its horrid throne and keeps its seat with force of arms so that its empire is undisturbed. In others, the throne is disputed, for the conscience mutinies, but yet the tyrant is not dethroned. Over the whole world, sin exercises a dreadful tyranny. It would hold us in the same bondage were it not for One who is stronger than sin who has undertaken to deliver us out of its hand. Here is the charter of our liberty, the security of our safety: "Sin shall not have dominion over you."

Chapter One

Believers Free from
the Power of Sin

For sin shall not have dominion over you: for ye are not under the law, but under grace—Romans 6:14.

THE APOSTLE PAUL was absolutely clear in his description of living the Christian life: "Neither yield ye your members as instruments of unrighteousness unto sin: but yield yourselves unto God" (Romans 6:13). It is both the way *to* peace and the way *of* peace to submit one's whole self to God. Nor is it a difficult task to a true believer, but it is the desire of his heart, the pleasure of his life. The believer shudders at the idea of yielding his members as instruments of unrighteousness unto sin, but he yields himself to God as one who has been made alive from the dead and his members as instruments of righteousness to God. Complete consecration of every faculty of mind and body to the Lord is our soul's deepest wish. We can sing most sincerely that sweet consecration hymn:

> Take my hands and let them move,
> At the impulse of thy love.
> Take my feet and let them be,
> Swift and beautiful for thee.

Take my voice and let me sing,
Always, only for my King:
Take my lips and let them be,
Filled with messages from thee.

Take my will and make it thine,
It shall be no longer mine.
Take my intellect, and use
Every power as thou shalt choose.

So that all my powers combine,
To adore thy grace divine,
Heart and soul a living flame,
Glorifying thy great name.

But we find another law in our members that wars against the law of our mind. To the full yielding up of all our members we find a hindrance in the sin that dwells in us, that sin that finds its haunt and hiding place in the desires, passions, and appetites of our flesh. These desires are right enough within proper limits. It is right, for example, that we eat and drink, but our natural instincts are apt to demand indulgence and so to become lusts. Our mortal body in its natural desires affords dens for the foxes of sin. The carnal mind also readily leans to the indulgence of the body, and thus there is presented a powerful opposition to the work of grace. Every child of God is conscious of the presence of the rebellious power and principle of sin within him. We strive to keep it under, to subdue and conquer it, and we hope to see it utterly exterminated at the last. Our case is like that of Israel with the Canaanites, and we long for the day when "there shall be no more the Canaanite in the house of the LORD of hosts" (Zech. 14:21).

Sin is a domineering force. No one can sin up to a fixed point and then say to sin, "This is as far as you go." Sin is an imperious power, and where it dwells it is hungry for the mastery. Just as our Lord, when He enters the soul, will never be content with a divided dominion, so is it with sin. Sin labors to bring our entire personality under subjection. Hence, we are compelled to strive daily against this ambitious principle. According to the working of the Spirit of God in us, we wrestle against sin that it may not have dominion over us. Sin has unquestioned dominion over multitudes of human hearts, and in some it has set up its horrid throne and keeps its seat with force of arms so that its empire is undisturbed. In others, the throne is disputed, for the conscience mutinies, but yet the tyrant is not dethroned. Over the whole world, sin exercises a dreadful tyranny. It would hold us in the same bondage were it not for One who is stronger than sin who has undertaken to deliver us out of its hand. Here is the charter of our liberty, the security of our safety: "Sin shall not have dominion over you." Sin reigns over those who abide in unbelief, but it shall not have dominion over *you*, "because greater is he that is in you, than he that is in the world" (1 John 4:4).

If we are distressed by the fear that sin will ultimately get the mastery over us, let us be comforted by our text. Holy jealousy leads us to fear that though we have for many years been enabled to maintain a spotless character before men, we may in some unguarded hour make shipwreck of faith and end our life voyage as castaways upon the rocks of shame. The flesh is frail and our strength is perfect weakness, and therefore we dread lest we should make some terrible fall and bring dishonor upon the holy name by which we are called. Under such feelings we may fly for comfort to the rich assurance of the text, "Sin shall not have dominion over you."

Three things demand our consideration and afford us consolation. The first is *the peculiar position* of believers—"Ye are not under the law, but under grace." Second, the *special assurance* made to believers, "Sin shall not have dominion over you." And third, *the remarkable reason* given for this statement, "Sin shall not have dominion over you: for ye are not under the law, but under grace."

A Peculiar Position

"Ye are not under the law." All men are under the law by nature, and consequently they are condemned by it because they have broken its commands. Apart from our Lord Jesus, men are only criminals under sentence and waiting for the appointed hour when the warrant shall be solemnly executed upon them. But believers are regarded as having died in Christ, and by that death they have escaped from under the law. Believers are delivered from the law by the fact that their Redeemer endured the penalty of the law on their behalf and at the same time honored the law by rendering perfect obedience to it. All the law's requirements have been met, so that it has no more demands upon His people.

"Not under the law" means that we are not trying to be saved by obedience to law. We do not pretend to earn eternal life by merit or hope to claim anything of the Lord as due to us for good works. We do not expect to earn a reward, neither are we flogged to duty by dread of punishment. We are under grace—that is to say, we are treated on the principle of mercy and love and not on that of justice. Freely, of His own undeserved favor, God has forgiven us for Christ's sake. He has regarded us with favor, not because we deserved it, but simply because He willed to do so according to that ancient declaration, "I will have mercy on whom I will have mercy, and I will have compassion on whom I will have compassion" (Rom. 9:15). Moreover, our continuance in a state of salvation depends upon the same grace that first placed us there. We do not stand or fall according to our personal merit, but because Jesus lives, we live, because Jesus is accepted, we are accepted, because Jesus is beloved, we are beloved. In a word, our standing is based not upon merit but upon mercy, not upon our changeable character but upon the immutable mercy of God. Grace is the tenure upon which we hold our position before the Lord. "For by grace are ye saved through faith; and that not of yourselves: it is the gift of God" (Eph. 2:8). "But that no man is justified by the law in the sight of God, it is evident: for, The just shall live by faith. And the law is not of faith: but, The man that doeth them shall live in them" (Gal. 3:11–12).

Let us endeavor to recount the privileges of this position by mentioning the evils from which it releases us. First, *we no longer dread the curse of the law.* Those who are under the law may well be horribly afraid because of the penalties that are due through their many failures and transgressions. They have broken the law and are therefore in constant danger of judgment and condemnation. The careless try to shake off the thought as much as possible by putting off the evil day, by forgetting death, and by pretending to disbelieve in judgment and eternal wrath. But still more or less this thought disturbs them; a dreadful sound is in their ears. When men are once awakened, the dread of punishment for sin haunts them day and night, filling them with terror. And well it may, for they are under the law, and the law will soon cast them into its prison, from which they will never escape. Every transgression and disobedience must receive a just recompense of reward.

Believers have no fear as to the punishment of their sin, for our sin was by the Lord Himself laid upon Jesus, and the penalty was borne by Him: "the chastisement of our peace was upon him; and with his stripes we are healed" (Isa. 53:5). "Christ hath redeemed us from the curse of the law, being made a curse for us: for it is written, Cursed is every one that hangeth on a tree" (Gal. 3:13). Substitution clears the Christian from all debt to justice, and the believer dares to challenge the law itself with the question,Who is he that condemns, since Christ has died? Then he goes further and challenges an accusation: "Who shall lay any thing to the charge of God's elect? It is God that justifieth" (Rom. 8:33). No penalty do we dread, for we are forgiven, and God will not pardon and then punish. "As far as the east is from the west, so far hath he removed our transgressions from us" (Ps. 103:12). When we see the stern array of the judgment seat and hear the threatenings of justice, we who are believers rejoice to feel that these terrors have nothing to do with us. The Great Surety has secured His people from all risk of wrath. The unquenchable fire is not for them, neither shall the pit close its mouth upon them, for they are not under the law.

Then the believer *no longer drudges in unwilling obedience, seeking to reach a certain point of merit.* The man under the law very frequently tries to keep the commands to attain a fair measure of goodness. For this he labors very hard, as men who tug at the oar to escape from the tempest. If he could but reach a certain degree of virtue, he would feel safe. Alas, he has no power to attain even to his own idea. He finds his resolutions written in water, and his goodness vanishes like the morning mist. All the works in the world fail to yield him peace of mind. The believer is under no such drudgery. Christ has fulfilled the law for him, and the believer rests in that finished work. He does not aim at high attainments to win the favor of God, for he has that favor. The favor of God has come to him freely and undeservedly, and he rejoices in it. A high ambition moves him, but it is not that of saving himself by his own works. The believer obeys out of love, delighting in the law after the inner man and confessing with Paul, "the law is holy, and the commandment holy, and just, and good" (Rom. 7:12). He wishes that he could live without sin, but he never dreams that he could make atonement for the past, nor does he fancy that by his own merit he is to obtain salvation for the future. The work through which he is saved is complete—it is not his own work, but the work of Jesus. When he sees his own shortcomings and iniquities, he does not, therefore, doubt his salvation but continues to rest in Jesus. He is no longer a slave, flogged with the whip of fear and made to labor for his very life and gather nothing for his pains. He is free from the principle of law and works from a principle of love—not to secure divine favor but because that favor has been freely manifested toward him.

The Christian man is now *no longer uncertain as to the continuance of divine love*. Under the law, no man's standing can be secure, since by a single sin he may forfeit his position. If a legalist should be able to persuade himself that he has reached a sufficient point of merit and is safe, he still cannot be sure of continuing in his exalted position. However meritorious a man may conceive himself to be, yet he may fall short of the standard. Faith is the only way that we can tread, since all the good works we have ever done are defiled and polluted either in motive beforehand or in the spirit in which they were done or by proud reflections afterward. We dare not trust even our prayers and devotions and givings or repentances but must rest upon the merit of Christ alone. The merit of Christ is always a constant and abiding quantity. If, therefore, we rest thereon, our foundation is as secure at one time as at another. The merits of Jesus will be throughout eternity sweet before God on our behalf. "For if, when we were enemies, we were reconciled to God by the death of his Son, much more, being reconciled, we shall be saved by his life" (Rom. 5:10). We are clear from the bondage of the law, since we have come under the covenant of grace, which is founded upon promises that nothing can disannul.

In consequence of this the believer is *no longer afraid of the last great day*. Shall all our sins be read and published before an assembled universe? "If so," says the man who is under the law, "it will go hard for me." Judgment is a terrible word to those who are hoping to save themselves, for if their doings are to be put into the balances, they will surely be found wanting. But judgment has no terror in it to a believer: the believer can sing with the poet:

Bold shall I stand in that last day,
For who aught to my charge shall lay?
While through thy blood absolved I am
From sin's tremendous curse and shame.

Will the sins of believers be published at the last day? If it is to the glory of forgiving love, let them be. Who among us need be afraid, since at the end of the whole list there shall be written, "And all these were blotted out for Jesus Christ's sake." And if they are not published because all our sins were cast behind Jehovah's back, and if instead the Judge shall only proclaim the good works of His people and say, "For I was an hungered, and ye gave me meat: I was thirsty, and ye gave me drink: . . . Inasmuch as ye have done it unto one of the least of these my brethren, ye have done it unto me" (Matt. 25:35, 40), then we may welcome the last judgment and cry, "Welcome, welcome, Son of God." If the book of record shall be opened that might justly condemn us, yet it is written, "and another book was opened, which is the book of life" (Rev. 20:12). If our names are there, we have nothing to fear.

One word may be added here, namely, that the believer being no longer under the law has *no slavish dread of God.* As long as I am at enmity with God, guilty of breaking His law and liable to His righteous wrath, I dread His name and shrink from His presence. The soul under the law stands as the Israelites did, far off from the mountain, with a boundary set between themselves and the glory of God (Ex. 20:18). Distance and separation are the natural condition of all who are under the law. Not so the believer, for his heart and his flesh cry out for the Lord, and he pants to come and appear before God. We have access with boldness to the throne of heavenly grace, and we delight to avail ourselves of it. Through the Mediator we have fellowship with the Father and His Son Jesus Christ. The Holy Ghost has made us long to be brought nearer and nearer to our divine Father. Our God is a consuming fire (Heb. 12:29), but that consuming fire has no terror for us, since it will only melt the alloy from the gold and remove the dross from the silver. The law could only say to us, "Depart, ye cursed," but grace says, "Come, ye blessed." We have accepted the call of grace, and now we know the Lord and love him. "Perfect love casteth out fear: because fear hath torment" (1 John 4:18).

I beg you to understand this freedom from the law and then to hold it fast, for there are some who return in a measure to the legal yoke. The apostle says, "Stand fast therefore in the liberty wherewith Christ hath made us free, and be not entangled again with the yoke of bondage" (Gal. 5:1). Do you feel helpless, cold, and heavy and therefore conclude that you are not saved? Are you not coming under the law and measuring the power of the grace of God by your own deservings and excellencies? If you judge your standing before God by anything except your faith in His promise, you will bring yourself into bondage. You can walk by faith, but you will stumble if you try any other way. When Satan says, "You are no saint," do not argue with him, for he is too subtle for a poor soul like you. Yield the point and say, "If I am not a saint, I am a sinner; and being a sinner, I find it written that Christ Jesus came into the world to save sinners. I put myself on that list, O Satan, and even you cannot deny that I am such. I believe in Jesus, and believing in Him I am justified before God by the righteousness of my Lord, and I have peace with God through Jesus Christ." This is safe standing. If we are indeed saved by the righteousness of another, why do we question the power of that righteousness to save us because of our own conscious feebleness? We are saved not by our own strength or feebleness but by the power of the Lord Jesus. If we are standing with one foot on the rock of Christ's finished work and the other upon the sand of our own doings, we may well stand or totter according to which foot we are trusting to. But if we set both feet upon the rock, we may stand fast though the sea roar and the floods sweep the sand away. Do not try the double foundation, for it will never answer. Partly Christ and partly self will soon come to failure. No, our great Redeemer cried, "It is finished," and it *is* finished, and those who rest on Him have a finished salvation, for they are not under the law but under grace.

The Special Assurance

"Sin shall not have dominion over you." *This is a very needful assurance*, especially at times. Sin is a great working power, and all around us we see its hideous operations. It is an evil as incessant in its activity as it is deadly in its results. As we look at its forcible workings, we cry in alarm, "It will surely drag me down one of these days," but the dread fear is removed by the cheering voice of the Holy Ghost, who assures us, "Sin shall not have dominion over you."

Alas, not only do we see the evil working in others, but evil assails us. Our eyes are drawn aside to look on vanity, our ears to hear evil speaking, and our heart itself at times grows cold and wanders. Then we are apt to be cast down and to doubt. Here the sweet assurance cheers us—though you are tempted, you shall not be led astray, for "sin shall not have dominion over you." "Resist the devil, and he will flee from you" (James 4:7). Stand in the strength of faith and in the power of the precious blood, and though you are beset with evil suggestions a thousand times a day and every sense is assailed by the witcheries of evil, yet "sin shall not have dominion over you." Cheered by such a word as this, we remain on our watchtower and are not overcome of evil.

Sometimes sin forces its way into our souls and rouses our inward desires to an awful degree so that the imagination sets fire to our lusts and the smoke of the conflagration blows in the eyes of the affections and almost chokes the understanding. Yes, sin may invade your soul so as to be your plague and torment. Sin may crush you down, rob you of your comfort, injure your graces, and wreak havoc upon your peace, but it shall not have dominion over you. Those of you who are acquainted with John Bunyan's *Holy War* will remember how wonderfully the glorious dreamer describes Diabolus besieging the town of Mansoul after it had been occupied by the Prince Immanuel. After many battles and cunning plots, the enemy entered into the city, filling the streets with the yells of his followers and polluting the whole place with the presence of his hosts. But yet he could not take the castle in the center of the town, which held out for Immanuel. That castle was the heart, and the enemy could by no means secure a footing in it. He beat his big hell drum almost day and night around the walls, but he could not enter. No, sin may for a while seem to prevail in the believer till he has no rest, hearing nothing but the devil's whisper in his ears—"Sin, sin, sin"—but nevertheless sin shall not have dominion over him. Sin may haunt your home and follow you down the streets in your walks, entering the very room into which you withdraw to pray, but your inmost self shall still cry out against it, for "sin shall not have dominion over you." Sin may trouble you and thrust itself upon you, but it cannot become your lord. The devil has great wrath and rages horribly for a while, knowing that his time is short (Rev. 12:12), but he shall be subdued and expelled, for the Lord our God gives us the victory through Jesus Christ.

Sometimes, alas, sin even prevails over us, and we are forced in deep anguish to confess that we have fallen beneath its power. It is terrible that it should be so, even for a moment, and yet it would be a lie to deny the mournful fact. Who among us can say, "I am clean, I have not sinned"? Still, a temporary defeat is not sufficient to effect a total subjugation. Sin shall not have dominion over the believer, for though he falls, he shall rise again. The child of God when he falls into the mire is like the sheep that gets up and escapes from the ditch as quickly as possible; it is not his nature to lie there. The ungodly man is like the hog that rolls in the filth and wallows in it with delight. The mire has dominion over the swine, but it has none over the sheep. With many bleatings and outcries the sheep seeks the shepherd again, but not so the swine. Every child of God weeps, mourns, and bemoans his sin, and he hates it when for a while he has been overtaken by it. Sin has an awful power, but it has no dominion; it casts us down, but it cannot make us take delight in its evil.

There are times when the believer feels intensely his danger. "My feet were almost gone; my steps had well nigh slipped" (Ps. 73:2). Then how sweetly does this assurance come to the soul: "Sin shall not have dominion over you." The Lord is able to keep you from falling, and you shall be preserved even to the end (Jude 24).

This assurance secures us from a very great danger—from the danger of being under the absolute sway of sin. What is meant by sin having dominion? Look around and see. There are men who live in sin, and yet they do not appear to know it. Sin has dominion over them by spreading a veil over their hearts so that their conscience is deadened. They are so enslaved as to be content in bondage. You shall not be so enslaved. You shall be so enlightened and instructed that when you sin you shall be well aware of it. Self-excuse shall be impossible to you. God has so changed your nature by His grace that when you sin you shall be like a fish on dry land; you shall be out of your element. You cannot drink sin down as the ox drinks down water, but to you it shall be as the brine of the sea.

You may become so foolish as to try the pleasures of the world, but they shall be no pleasures to you. You shall cry out with Solomon, "Vanity of vanities; all is vanity" (Eccl. 1:2). That marvelous man tried the world at its best and was disappointed, and you may be quite sure that where he failed you will not succeed.

Sin will never yield you satisfaction. In worldly company you shall feel like a man who sits upon thorns or walks amid snakes, and in worldly amusement you shall feel as if the house shall fall upon you. You shall never be made happy by evil but shall groan under it if you ever yield to its power. You shall hate yourself to think you ever consented to its solicitations. You shall be wretched and unhappy and shall find no rest till you return unto your Lord. If you are a believer in Christ, you must fight with sin till you die, and what is more, you must conquer it in the name of Christ. You are sometimes afraid that it will vanquish you, but if you are of the true seed, it cannot prevail. Like Samson, you shall break all its bands. You shall rise superior to habits that now enthrall you; you shall even forget those strong impulses that now sweep you before them. Your inward graces shall gather force, while the Holy Spirit shall help your weaknesses and you shall be changed from glory to glory as by the presence of the Lord.

This assurance is confirmed by the context: "Sin shall not have dominion over you," because you are dead to it by virtue of your union to Christ. You died with Christ, and you have been buried with Christ. How then shall sin have dominion over you? Besides, you live in Christ in newness of life by reason of His living in you. How can the new nature live in sin? How can that which is born of God live like that which is born of the devil? No, no, it cannot be. Christ has undertaken to save you from your sins, and He will do it. He will help you by His Spirit. He will perfect you in Himself. You are bound for victory, and you shall have it. Thanks be to God who gives it to you through Jesus Christ our Lord. "Sin shall not have dominion over you."

The Remarkable Reason

"For ye are not under law, but under grace." "There, there," says many an unconverted man, "so then we are not under law!

Well, then, we may sin as we like." That is the way in which a base heart sours the sweet milk of the Word, but it is not the argument of the child of God. Mark how Paul puts it: "What shall we say then? Shall we continue in sin, that grace may abound? God forbid" (Rom. 6:1–2). Paul flings away the inference with horror and detestation. Let me just show you why being under the law is not helpful to holiness, while being under grace is the great means to it.

Those who are under the law will always be under the dominion of sin, and it cannot be otherwise. First, the law puts a man under the dominion of sin by pronouncing sentence of condemnation upon him as soon as he has transgressed. What does the law say to him? "You are guilty, and I condemn you. He that offends in one point is guilty of all." Thus the law shuts a man up to being a sinner and offers him no space for repentance. It accuses, condemns, and sentences but affords no hope. It is not so with those who are under grace. To them, grace is, "You are sinners, but you are freely forgiven; go and sin no more." Thus relieved, the penitent lifts up his head and cries, "Enable me to pray to You and grant that I may be upheld by grace in the way of uprightness." The amazing love of God when shed abroad in the heart creates a desire for better things, and what the law could not do, grace accomplishes.

A man under the law is by the law driven to despair. A person says, "Am I to keep this law in order to be saved? Alas, I have already broken it!" Therefore, he resolves that he will not attempt the task, and he sinks into indifference, or in some cases, he resolves that he will take his fill of sin. Because there is no hope, he will plunge into iniquity. He vows that if hell must be his portion forever, he will enjoy the sweetness there is in sin while he may. So the law, because of the evil heart it has to deal with, excites such a condition of heart that sin is confirmed in its dominion. Being threatened, the rebellious heart hardens itself and defies the Lord; and then concluding that peace is impossible, it continues more and more to fight against the Lord. Not so the child of God, who says, "God, for Christ's sake, has cast my sins behind His back, and I am saved. Now, because of love I bear His name. I will serve Him with all my might, because of all that He has done for me." Thus the grace of our Lord Jesus, by its freeness and richness breaks the dominion of sin that the law only served to establish and confirm, not that the law is evil, but because we are evil and rebel against the holy law.

A man under the law does not escape from the dominion of sin because *the law rouses the opposition of the human heart.* There are a great many things that people never think of doing till they are forbidden. Lock up a closet in your house and say to your children, "You must never enter that closet or even look into the keyhole." Perhaps they have never wanted to look into the dingy old closet before, but now they can hardly wait to inspect it. Law, by reason of our unruly nature, excites opposition and creates sin, for what a man may not do he immediately wants to do. He who is under the law will never escape from the dominion of sin, for sin comes by the law by reason of the iniquities of our hearts. But when we are under grace, we love God for His love for us and labor to please Him in all things.

The law moreover offers a man no actual help. All it does is to say, "Thou shalt" and "Thou shalt not." It can do no more. But grace gives us what the law requires of us. The law says, "Make you a new heart"; grace replies, "A new heart also will I give you, and a new spirit will I put within you" (Ezek. 36:26). The law says, "Keep my commandments"; and grace answers, "Thou shalt keep my commandments and do them." Grace brings the Holy Spirit into the soul to work in us holy desires and a hatred of sin, and hence what the law could not do, in that it was weak through the flesh, grace accomplishes for us by its own almighty power (Rom. 8:3).

Further, the law inspires no sentiment of love, and love, after all, is the fulfilling of the law (Gal. 5:14). If you are told you shall and you shall not, there is nothing in this to inspire love to the lawgiver. Law is hard and cold, like the two tablets of Moses. Law never excites enthusiasm for that which is right; it is too stern and chill to touch the heart. Mere law does not ever raise in a man's heart a high ideal of what the man should be. Look at the legalist: he looks upon religion as a task in which he has no delight. He does as much or as little as he is forced to do, but his heart is not in it. Those who think they have kept the law of God are evidently very far from understanding its meaning: they have a very poor idea of the mind of God, or they would not have thought that they had fulfilled the will of God with such a poor, miserable, hypocritical righteousness as theirs. The Pharisee had formed a shockingly low notion of true holiness; in fact, he degraded the law into a mere external ordinance, taking note of the outside of the cup and platter and leaving the inside full of filthiness (Matt. 23:26). But see what grace does. It fires a man with enthusiasm and sets before him a lofty idea of excellence. It causes him to love the Lord, and then it gives him a high idea of purity and holiness. Though he rises many grades beyond the Pharisee, yet the believer cries, "I am not what I should be." And if he becomes the most zealous, consecrated man that ever lived, the law is still beyond him, and he still asks that he may be able to rise to greater heights of holiness and virtue. This grace does, but this the law can never do.

The most pleasing service in the world is that which is done from motives of love and not for wages. The mere legalist does what he should, or at least thinks he does; but as for heartiness and zeal, he knows nothing of such things. The child of God, with all his feebleness and blunderings, is far more accepted, for he does all he can out of pure love, and then still cries, "I am an unprofitable servant. I have done no more than was my duty to have done. The Lord help me to do more." God accepts heart service, but heart service the law never did produce, and never will. The only true heart service in the world comes from those who are not under the law but are under grace; hence, sin shall not have dominion over those who are not under the law.

The spirit of the world is legal, and the world's wisemen tell us that we must preach that people must be virtuous or they will go to hell, holding out heaven as the reward for morality. They believe in the principle of chain and whip. But what comes of such doctrine? The more you preach it, the less virtue, the less obedience there is in the world. But when you preach love, the effect is very different. "Come," the Lord says, "I forgive you freely. Trust my Son, and I will save you outright, though in you there is nothing to merit My esteem. Accept My free favor, and I will receive you graciously and love you freely." This looks at first sight as if it gives a license to sin, but how does it turn out? Why, this wondrous grace taking possession of the human heart breeds love in return, becoming the fountain of purity and holiness, and such as receive it endeavor to perfect holiness in the fear of God (2 Cor. 7:1).

Do not get under the law, do not yield to legal threats or legal hopes, but live under the free grace gospel. Let the note that peals on your ear be no longer the thunder of Sinai, but let it be the sweet song of free grace and dying love. Ah, ring those charming bells from morning till evening. Let us hear their liquid music again and again. Live and do, not do and live.

Many people are violent against one sin, but the true saint abhors all sin. You may not allow the sin of drunkenness to have dominion over you, but are you selfish and ungenerous? What have you done? You have only changed your idols. You have dethroned one usurper to set up another. If you were once profane and are now hypocritical, you have only changed iniquities. It is a very curious thing how one sin feeds on another: the death of profligacy may be the resurrection of greed; the flight of pride may be the advent of shameless folly. The man who was lewd, riotous, and brawling has killed those sins, and on their graves he has sown a handful of poisonous weed called pride, and it flourishes amazingly. It may be London pride, country pride, English pride, or American pride, but it is rare stuff to grow, and to grow over the rotting carcasses of other sins. Unbelief may dethrone superstition, but its own reign may be no real improvement upon that of credulity. If you only throw down Baal to set up Ashtaroth, what progress have you made toward God? Little does it signify which of the false gods is set up in the temple of Jehovah, for He hates them all. The right prayer is, "Let not any iniquity have dominion over me."

Chapter Two

A Passion for Holiness

I opened my mouth, and panted: for I longed for thy command-
ments. Look thou upon me, and be merciful unto me, as thou usest
to do unto those that love thy name. Order my steps in thy word:
and let not any iniquity have dominion over me—Psalm 119:131–
133.

I KNOW THAT whenever the truth of holi-
ness is presented in an understandable manner, many desires after
holiness are stimulated. It should be so as soon as the truth is received into the mind. Note the verse that precedes the quoted text:
"The entrance of thy words giveth light; it giveth understanding
unto the simple." Then note that the next step is intensity of desire:
"I opened my mouth, and panted: for I longed for thy commandments." When we have light enough to see what holiness is and
how desirable it is, we should hunger and thirst after it. To be holy,
to have a desire for holiness, to labor and agonize for actual holiness of life, is the desire of God's good Spirit for our attainment.

Here we have David desiring, praying, and pleading for, and
setting forth very clearly what he pants and thirsts after. May you
and I have the same burning desires. And at the same time may
we clearly know what we are panting for so that we may pursue
it more intelligently and thus go the shortest path to obtain it! May

the Holy Spirit, the author of holiness, help us as we consider these three verses!

In the first verse you have the psalmist *longing intently after holiness*: "I opened my mouth, and panted: for I longed for thy commandments." In the next verse you have David *pleading fervently for the thing that he desired*, praying in this fashion: "Look thou upon me, and be merciful unto me, as thou usest to do unto those that love thy name." In the third verse you have the same man of God *enlarging intelligently upon what it was that he pleaded for*, giving both the positive and the negative side of it: "Order my steps in thy word: and let not any iniquity have dominion over me."

Longing Passionately for the Lord's Commandments

"I opened my mouth, and panted: for I longed for thy commandments." Observe carefully that *the man of God longed for the Lord's commandments*. This can only mean that he longed to know them, longed to keep them, longed to teach them, longed to bring all around him into obedience to them. Many believers long after the promises, and that is good, but they must not forget to have an equal longing for the commandments. It is a sad sign when a person cannot bear to hear of the precepts but must always have the preacher touching the string of privileges. To the renewed man it is a privilege to receive a command from the Lord whom he serves and a great grace to have the will and the power to obey. To us grace means a power that sways us as well as a favor that distinguishes us. To me the greatest privilege in all the world would be perfect holiness. If I had my choice of all the blessings I can conceive of, I would choose perfect conformity to the Lord Jesus. I do not think I would have made Solomon's choice of wisdom, unless it included wisdom of moral and spiritual character—and that is holiness.

No unrenewed heart ever sighed and cried after holiness. A mere passing wish is of little worth: I am speaking of the intense and continual desire of the heart. We must strive after holiness with an agony of desire. Oh, to be rid of every sin! What is that but heaven? Oh, to escape from every tendency and trace of sin! This would be bliss. What more of happiness could we desire than to fulfill that word of our Lord—"Be ye therefore perfect, even as your Father which is in heaven is perfect" (Matt. 5:48)? Are you conscious of great longings to escape from sin? Do you feel far less dread of hell than of sin? Is sin the worst of hells to you? Is it horrible, terrible, killing? Would it be the heaviest punishment that could be laid upon you if the Great Judge should say, "You are filthy; be filthy still. You are unholy; be unholy still"? It would certainly be the worst of deaths to some of us.

The deepest prayer of our heart is to be delivered from that sin that is the tinder in which the sparks of temptation find their fuel. We long to be delivered from that law in our members that brings us into captivity to sin. Oh, that we could be like Him who said, "The prince of this world cometh, and hath nothing in me" (John 14:30)! How wonderful! "Nothing in me"! Alas, the evil prince finds very much of his own in most of us! One of the best men I ever knew said at eighty years of age, "I find the old man is not dead yet." Our old man is crucified, but he is long a-dying. He is not dead when we think he is. You may live to be very old, but you have need still to watch against the carnal nature that remains even in the regenerate. I heard one speak about feeling angry when provoked, and he said he felt "a bone of the old man moving." Alas, there is more than a bone of it in us! There is the whole body of this death still left, and very substantial it does seem to be at times, so that we are forced to cry out, "O wretched man that I am! who shall deliver me from the body of this death?" (Rom. 7:24). We need deliverance, not from the bones of it, but from the very body of it that still plagues us. In those longings you see which way the stream of your heart is flowing. These desires, I say, show that you have a clean heart and a right spirit, a spirit that would do good, though evil is present with you. The tide is running in the right way, though the wind may be blowing against it. Being born of God, you do not commit sin as the tenor of your life, but you strive after that which is good and pure.

Observe the psalmist, having told us what he longed for, *shows the strength of those desires,* for he had been so eager in his pursuit of holiness that he had lost his breath. He could not find among men a good figure to describe himself, so he looked among the animals and selected the panting stag as his crest. The hart has been hunted over hill and dale, the dogs long close behind it. It has fled, as with the wings of a swift eagle, from their murderous teeth. For a moment the stag has eluded them. It pauses, longing to bathe itself in the water brook. It is hot and weary and thirsty and therefore opens wide its mouth. See how it pants! Mark how its breast heaves and its whole body palpitates while it tries to regain its breath! The poor hunted thing is exhausted with its desperate efforts. Have not we also at times felt spent in the struggle against sin? We have said to ourselves, "What more can we do? This fierce temptation returns. We may yet be overthrown by it. Oh, that we could take to ourselves wings and fly away! Woe to us, for we have no strength."

You were like a man who is out of breath, striving beyond yourself after "life more abundantly." Accursed is that man who has exhausted body and mind in the race of sin. From that curse he can escape only by looking to Jesus, who was made a curse for us. But blessed is that man who has spent all the energy of his being in following after righteousness, for out of weakness he shall be made strong. When he cries, "My foot slippeth" (Ps. 38:16), the mercy of the Lord shall hold him up. When, like David in the battle with the giant, he waxes faint, the Lord shall cover his head. Meanwhile he opens his mouth and pants out his weariness, but the Lord is with him, and He will preserve him alive. Are you ready to faint even now? Underneath are the everlasting arms. He who faints in such a pursuit as this shall swoon away upon the bosom of his Lord. Be of good comfort.

See, next, *how resolved he was.* He says, "I opened my mouth, and panted." He is eager to go onward. Worn out by previous effort, he does not lie down to die but is determined to still be on the move. Give up the struggle? Never! We have drawn the sword against the Canaanites of sin, and we will never sheathe it until the last of them is slain. It may be a lifelong battle, but we will never make a truce or treaty with sin. Woe to him who says of holiness, "This is as far as you shall come, but no further, and here shall your proud waves be held." We must never degrade ourselves by saying, "This sin cannot be conquered, for it is constitutional: as it was bred in my bone it must be allowed to come out in my flesh." We allow no excuse for ourselves. We will not plead for the life of a single sin.

Oh, for the holy fury of a sanctified breaker of images, who will spare nothing that is opposed to God! We are called to break in pieces every idol, to cast down every grove, and to overthrow every altar so that Jehovah may be God alone in the land. I charge you, abhor the idea of compromise with error and with evil. If you say, "I will only sin so far," you might as well say, "I will only take so much poison or stab myself a few inches deep." Alas, you have given up the fight when you have come to terms with the foe! A hot temper may be natural, but it must be conquered. A miserly spirit may be inborn, but it must be cast out. A proud mind may be a family heritage, but it must be laid low. Certain weeds may be indigenous to the soil of your nature, and therefore it may be doubly difficult to eliminate them, but the work must be done. Keep the hoe going; never cease from the determination to uproot the last of the weeds. Even though you open your mouth and pant with weariness, yet keep your face set like a flint toward holiness and let your case be that of one who is "faint, yet pursuing."

Note that the follower after holiness *seeks renewed strength.* Why does he open his mouth and pant? Is it not to get more air, to fill his lungs again, to cool his blood, and to be ready to renew his running? When you have an hour's rest from the battle against sin, spend it in furbishing your shield and sharpening your sword, for another assault will soon be upon you. We *can* become strong again. "He giveth more grace" (James 4:6). We are never for a moment to suppose that we have exhausted the strength of God when we have exhausted our own. We should be all the more earnest to draw upon divine all-sufficiency. We are to be like that fabled giant, whom Hercules could not overcome for a long while because he was a child of the earth, and every time he was thrown down he touched his mother earth and rose with fresh strength. Now, whenever you are thrown down and touch your God in your faintness and weakness, you will find that He restores your soul: "To them that have no might he increaseth strength" (Isa. 40:29). When cast down we cry, "Rejoice not against me, O mine enemy: when I fall, I shall arise" (Micah 7:8).

"When I am weak, then am I strong" (2 Cor. 12:10). May we realize the truth of that Christian paradox! *We can* overcome sin in the power of the Lord. The Canaanites have chariots of iron, but Christ has a rod of iron with which He can break them in pieces. Sin is strong, but grace is stronger. Satan is wise, but God is all-wise. The Lord is on our side; therefore let us open our mouth wide and take in another draught of heaven's reviving air; let us bathe in the water of life; let us drink from the smitten rock; and in thus waiting upon the Lord we shall renew our strength. Has He not said, "Open thy mouth wide, and I will fill it" (Ps. 81:10)? When our desires are after the best things, we may expect the Lord to meet with us and grant us times of refreshing from His presence. In remembrance of these visitations and the time of intense desire that preceded them, we can say, "I opened my mouth, and panted: for I longed for thy commandments."

The psalmist was *dissatisfied with his attainments.* May we never be content with ourselves. We are satisfied with the Word of God; we are satisfied with the gospel of God; we are satisfied with the favor of God; we are satisfied with the Christ of God; but we shall never be satisfied with our own personal condition till we wake up in the likeness of the Firstborn Son. Satisfaction with self is the death of progress. He who is not content with his place in the race will push forward, but he who is proud of his position in the running will soon tire and fall behind. Like the man on the bicycle, we must keep going; to stop is to drop. On! On! On! You are only safe as the wheel spins round and you throw the miles behind you. My text is not the utterance of one who is sitting in his chair with the motto on the wall behind him, "Rest and be thankful." As for the man who feels as the psalmist did, his mind is far away in the land beyond him. His opened mouth and panting heart represent desires that are not as yet fulfilled.

Yet, let no tinge of discouragement mingle with your dissatisfaction: *this man is hopeful of better things.* He opens his mouth because he looks for something to fill it; he pants because he believes in waterbrooks that will relieve his thirst. Wisemen will pant only for that which it is possible to attain. We do not shoot at the moon or aim at an absurd ideal. We are not even rash, like those who seek the North Pole and risk their lives for a dream. God can make us holy. Few of us have an adequate idea of what we may become even here by divine grace. The possibilities of sanctification are seldom explored, but most believers are content with small things in this direction. When a man asks me, "Can I be perfect?" and looks as if he would lead me into a debate upon the subject, I try to find out what manner of man he is before I answer. If he is an angry man, a hard man, a proud man, or a lover of his own supremacy, I smile at the question as coming from him. I picture a person who slept under a hedge last night, whose pockets are full of emptiness, whose clothes would disgrace a rag-bag, and this man wishes to discuss with me the question, Is great wealth attainable by an ordinary working man? I cannot see what the question has to do with him. When you are not doing what you might do, why speculate about what is possible or impossible? When a man has not enough grace to make change for a dollar, he may waive all questions about the millions of spiritual perfection. Do you cry, "Can I be perfect?" Have faith in God and say in His name, "If perfect holiness is possible, I will have it. If it can reached on earth, I will reach it." All that the Spirit of God can make out of such a poor sinner as I am it is my desire that He should make. I gladly submit myself and all that I have to His gracious operation. I would like to hear you say, "I must rise to a higher condition. I must be more Christlike. I must have less and less of self." May we be burning with an insatiable desire to be holy, and may we say with the inspired penman, "I opened my mouth, and panted: for I longed for thy commandments."

Pleading Fervently for Holiness

Desire, where it is real, will soon embody itself in prayer. Hence, we find the psalmist's breathings: "Look thou upon me, and be merciful unto me, as thou usest to do unto those that love thy name" (Ps. 119:132). You see, *he believes in God's power to bless him*, and hence he turns to Him and cries, "Look unto me." Is that all? Is a look sufficient? Is it not written, "Look unto me, and be ye saved" (Isa. 45:22)? That is our look to God. If our looking to God saves us, what will God's looking at us do? If there is so much power received by the eye of faith, how much will be given by the glance of love from God? Think not little of a look from God. A look—only a look! Ay, but it is from HIM. Remember what a look from Christ did for Peter. He did but look on Peter, and swearing

Peter turned to weeping Peter in a moment. Great sinners may be grateful for a look, for it is more than they deserve. Great saints may rejoice in a look, for it means much when the eye that looks is the eye of Omnipotent Love. "Look thou upon me." The favor of God is a choice means of sanctification. While affliction is greatly used of God to cleanse the heart, yet a very noble, soul-filling sense of the love of God is the truest sanctifier in the hand of the Holy Spirit. If you know that God loves you with an everlasting love, you will love the Lord and hate every false way. If you walk in the light of His countenance, you will walk in the way of His commandments. If God's love is shed abroad in your heart by the Holy Ghost, like sweet perfume, your life will be fragrant with it. It will become natural for you to please Him who loves you infinitely and immutably. Blessed is that man upon whom God looks with an eye of favorable regard. Lord, look on me and say by that look, "I have called thee by thy name; thou art mine" (Isa. 43:1), and this will cause me to keep in Your way! That is what the psalmist is here praying for. The Lord can sanctify us with a look of love. His choice makes us choice. His love fills us with love.

Observe that the pleader *appeals to mercy.* "Look thou upon me, and be merciful unto me." To be delivered from the power of sin is the greatest of mercies. Sin is a misery from which we can be saved only by mercy. "Be merciful unto me." We have no claim upon the Lord by way of merit; our appeal is to His sovereign grace. We have no rights—these we forfeited by our treason against our King. When you come before God in prayer, seeking sanctification, base your request upon His mercy: "Lord, You have done much for me; do still more and make me holy. I have not profited by Your discipline as I should have, but deal with me in patience. I am poor material for the potter's skill, but exercise Your longsuffering. Bear with me, and go on with Your work of grace until You have made me a vessel fit for Your use." It is truest, wisest, safest, for us to appeal to mercy. The best of saints are sinners still, and sinners always need mercy.

Then *he pleads as one who loves God.* He asks God to deal with him, saying, "As thou usest to do unto those that love thy name," implying that he is one of them. Do you love God's name, that is, His character and His revealed will? "Ay, that I do," cries one. "God is my exceeding joy, and I delight in His law after the inward man.

His holiness was once terrible to me, but now I admire and delight in it. Oh, that I were a partaker of it to the full!" You see the man's character by the way in which his heart takes its pleasure. If any man truly loves God, he will grow like God. The revealed character of God is to some of us a joy forever, and this is a sure mark of grace. We are not what we should be; we are not what we want to be; we are not what we hope to be; we are not what we shall be; but we do love the name of the Lord, and this is the root of the matter. We shall be like Him, for we love Him. Thus, the very fact that the Lord has filled us with love to Himself is a plea for further grace to keep His commandments.

The psalmist employs *the grand plea of use and wont*, for he says, "As thou usest to do unto those that love thy name." Use and wont generally have great weight in a court of law. Custom among men reaching far back holds good in court; how much shall the custom of the eternally unchanging God decide His future acts! The psalmist pleads the Lord's own custom, and this is a grand plea with Him, because He is unchanging. Whatever He has done He will do, and His having done it is a pledge that He will do it again, unless there is any declaration to the contrary. The psalmist seems to say, "You are in the habit of helping those who love Your name; Lord, help me. It is Your way to sanctify Your people; Lord, sanctify me. When saints desire to be holy, You are accustomed to grant their desire. Lord, grant mine, for I have the same desires." Is not this a good plea: "Be merciful to me, as thou usest to do unto those that love thy name"? If you think it a good idea, urge it at the throne of grace.

This involves another fact: *he joyfully accepts God's method*. When you cry to God to help you in your overcoming of sin, you must consent that He shall do it in His own way. If it is His will that sanctification should involve chastisement, are you willing? "Oh, yes!" you say, "Lord, do unto me as thou usest to do unto those that love thy name; and if it is written, 'As many as I love, I rebuke and chasten,' Lord rebuke and chasten me, so long as You do but love me." We assent to the processes of grace that we may enjoy the results of grace. It may so happen that if God sanctifies you, He may have to grind you very small: cheerfully yield yourself to the mill. If this is the way in which He deals with those who love His name, do not desire any different treatment. As a result, you may become a source for the ridicule of ungodly men, but do not complain, for this has frequently happened to those who love His name. God sanctifies His people, but not without their own effort in that direction. Be willing to make the effort, too.

Our prayer is that God would make us holy—holy through His favor, holy through His own gracious working—but we leave the methods in God's hands. Let God take His own way, His tried way, His ordinary way, His fixed way; only let Him deal mercifully with us. Let none of us demand exemption from the customary tests and trials. Do you expect to be crowned without warfare? Rewarded without labor? You expect what you will never have. Give up such idle dreams and plead the prayer of the text: "Look thou upon me, and be merciful unto me, as thou usest to do unto those that love thy name."

Enlarging Intelligently Upon the Favor He Seeks

When you go before God, it is good to know what you are in need of. Our older brethren used to say in prayer, "We would not rush into Your presence as the unthinking horse rushes into the battle." We must not go before God without thought and reverent preparedness of heart and mind.

Now, let us see how the psalmist puts it. His cry is for holiness, and *he describes it as being ruled by the Word of God.* "Order my steps in thy word." That is the reality of holiness. If we believe God's Word, we are orthodox; if we practice it, we are holy. The Bible is the great umpire as to conduct, and not the changing moral sentiment of passing generations. Pray God to order your life according to His Word. To this Word we must be conformed. This is our copy to write by; this is the image to which we must be modelled.

He would have holiness in every step of his life—"Order my steps in thy word." It is not, "Lord, order my journey as a whole," but, "Order my steps." We lose a great deal by lumping things; in the matter of holiness, detail is all important. Brethren, not only would I preach a holy sermon, but I desire that every word may be a holy word, every sentence a right sentence. As you believe in verbal inspiration for the Bible, so pray for verbal guidance in your speech and minute direction in your actions. The whole book of life will be excellent when every line and every letter is ordered according to the Word of the Lord. When we are careless as to the parts, we spoil the whole.

Notice that *he would have every step ordered.* "Order my steps." We wish to move the right foot first, but we must not take things for granted. We wish to put down the right foot in the right place, at the right time, with the right degree of force, and turn in the right direction. A great deal of holiness depends upon order, punctuality, and proportion. If order is not heaven's *first* law, it is certainly one of its laws; and proportion is another. Some men's lives are out of proportion. A man may be, in many points, a good man; you may say of him, bit by bit, "Yes, *that* is good, and *that* is good"; and yet he may have so much of one virtue that it may become a vice, and he may have so little of another virtue that it may be a grave defect. We can never attain to the right proportion of the virtues unless the Lord himself arranges them in order for us. Do not tell me it is easy to be holy: you need not only the different graces but also all of them in measured order. O Lord, help us! Order our steps.

We remark that *he would have every step full of God*: he would have each one ordered of the Lord. He would receive his strength, his motives, his guiding influences direct from the Lord: "Order my steps in thy word." Lord, when I put my foot down there, may it be at Your order; and when I move it to another place, may it still be at Your command. Let me go nowhere apart from Your divine guidance and command. "Well," cries one, "this is difficult." But although obedience may not be easy, it is free from the far greater difficulties that accompany self-will. A child who will do nothing but what his father commands does not find his course difficult; the difficulty comes in when he wants to follow his own will and to have his own way. You cannot serve God and self: if you try it, the mixture is nauseous and injurious. Say, "Lord, I would consult You about everything I think or say or do; for then that which I do will not have to be undone, that which I say will not be wished unsaid, and that which I think will not have to be wept over. 'Order my steps in thy word.' Put me under orders, keep me under orders, and never let me escape Your orders."

Observe that the last part of the verse is the negative way of describing holiness: "Let not any iniquity have dominion over me." *He would be wholly delivered from the tyranny of sin.* Many people are violent against one sin, but the true saint abhors all sin. You may not allow the sin of drunkenness to have dominion over you, but are you selfish and ungenerous? What have you done? You have only changed your idols. You have dethroned one usurper to set up another. If you were once profane and are now hypocritical, you have only changed iniquities. It is a very curious thing how one sin feeds on another: the death of profligacy may be the resurrection of greed; the flight of pride may be the advent of shameless folly. The man who was lewd, riotous, and brawling has killed those sins, and on their graves he has sown a handful of poisonous weed called pride, and it flourishes amazingly. It may be London pride, country pride, English pride, or American pride, but it is rare stuff to grow, and to grow over the rotting carcasses of other sins. Unbelief may dethrone superstition, but its own reign may be no real improvement upon that of credulity. If you only throw down Baal to set up Ashtaroth, what progress have you made toward God? Little does it signify which of the false gods is set up in the temple of Jehovah, for He hates them all. The right prayer is, "Let not any iniquity have dominion over me." Some sins are of respectable repute, and other sins are disreputable among men, but to a child of God, every sin is loathsome. Sins are all what Bunyan calls Diabolonians, and not one of them must be allowed to live in the town of Mansoul. I can see the throne set up within the heart of man. Who shall sit on it? It cannot be empty; who shall fill it? This sin, that sin, or the other? Nay, Lord, help me to keep every intruder out of it. Whether he comes as an angel of light or in his true character as the devil, help me to treat everyone as an enemy that would seek to supplant You in Your dominion over me. Oh, that God may reign over us from morning to evening, through every day of every week of every year!

"Let not any iniquity have dominion over me," is a prayer against the reign of sin. Sin will attack us, but sin shall not subdue us, for it is written, "Sin shall not have dominion over you" (Rom. 6:14). You may put up the sign: *Trespassers, Beware!* But the trespassers will come, do what you may; still they shall not be allowed to acquire a right-of-way through our nature. If a bird flies over our head, we cannot help it, but we will not let it make its nest in our hair. So a temptation may pass by us, an evil imagination may flit over the mind, but we will not invite evil, nor patiently endure it, nor allow it to lodge in our souls. Our bosom's throne is for the King of kings, Jesus, the Bridegroom of our hearts.

This is our prayer: "Let not any iniquity have dominion over us." I fear that many professing believers have never understood this prayer. One man is a splendid man for a prayer meeting, but at home he is a tyrant to his wife and children. Is not this a great evil under the sun? Another man is honest and strives with all his might against every form of evil, but he is hard even to cruelty with all who are in his power. One is good-natured and pleasant, but he adds extra to his bills at times and his customers do not find the goods quite of the quality they pay for. I have known a man who would not work on the Sabbath, but then he never worked on the other six days; and another who never broke the Sabbath, but he broke many hearts by his unkindness. Beware of pet sins. If you let a golden god rule you, you perish as quickly as if you let a mud god rule. Be this your constant cry: "Let not any iniquity have dominion over me."

In summary, the first thing you have to do is to see that you have these longings for holiness within you. If you have them, thank God for them. To pant after holiness is infinitely better than to be self-righteous. Cultivate these desires and cravings.

But never rest content with mere longings. He who really longs is not content to long: he desires to have his desire fulfilled. The only way to be holy is to go to a holy God through the holy Mediator. Trust in the atoning sacrifice of Jesus and so be reconciled to God by Him who alone can put away sin. Then go again to Jesus and ask Him to renew you in the spirit of your mind and wash you with water from the power of sin as He has washed you with blood from the guilt of it. When you are washed, take care that you keep your garments unspotted from the world. When you have once known the transforming power of the Holy Spirit, do not return again to folly. Follow on watchfully and resolutely. Seek the daily renewing of the Holy Spirit, and so shall you go from strength to strength till you shall be like your Lord and shall see Him as He is.

It is easy to find out others' faults and to bring the whole force of our mind to bear against them. It is delightful to expose vice and lampoon the follies of the age, adding a dash of wit to enliven it, or to preach virtue, with a little of the sugar of scandal to sweeten a painful tale. It highly gratifies some people when they can find a fault with some highly respected person. That is their forte, the strength of their genius, pulling to pieces what they could not put together and attempting to raise themselves by lowering others. But notice, the apostle says, "Let us cleanse ourselves." Oh, that we would all look at home! Oh, that we did more indoor work in this department! Our first business is to "cleanse ourselves." It is all very well to drag the church of God up to the altar like some bleeding victim, and there to stab her with the sharpest knife of our criticism and to say that she is not this and she is not that. One might rather ask, "How far do I help to make her what she is? If she is degenerate, how far is that degeneracy consequent upon my having fallen from the high standing that I should have occupied?" We shall all have contributed our quota to the reform of the church when we are ourselves reformed. There can be no better way of promoting general holiness than by increasing in personal holiness.

Chapter Three

Perfecting Holiness

Having therefore these promises, dearly beloved, let us cleanse ourselves from all filthiness of the flesh and spirit, perfecting holiness in the fear of God—2 Corinthians 7:1.

BURNING WITH STRONG EMOTION, constrained by the love of Christ, and animated by the fellowship of all spiritual blessings, the Apostle Paul here strikes out an exhortation that appeals to the noblest passions of the children of God—to their sense of a divine lineage, to the wonder of their present endowment, and to their exalted destiny—for an incentive to purity of character and holiness of life.

The Most Glorious Privileges

By such words as "Having therefore these promises," I understand not merely having the promises of an inheritance as they belonged to the Jews but also having received them, having obtained them, having grasped them, and being seized of them, as lawyers express it, so that the promises are no longer mere promises but things that we have actually in our possession. I understand by Paul's language that believers in the Lord Jesus Christ have a thousand blessed promises in the enjoyment of which they daily live.

The promises Paul especially refers to are mentioned in the previous chapter. The first promise is *divine indwelling*: "I will dwell in them" (2 Cor. 6:16). This is no light or inferior privilege of the Christian church. God has been pleased to make the bodies of His people to be the temples of the Holy Spirit. At this very moment, in every person who has put his trust in the Lord Jesus, Deity resides. He does not dwell in houses made with hands, that is to say, of man's building, but yet He dwells within these houses of clay, tabernacling in us. This is a promise that we have actually obtained and are now positively enjoying.

The next is *divine communion*: "I will dwell in them, and walk in them." As God talked with Abraham, so He does with every believer. God is not to us afar off, but He is our near and dear friend, our close acquaintance. If I can tell Him my heart, He also will tell me His heart, for "the secret of the LORD is with them that fear him" (Ps. 25:14). Communion is not merely a matter of promise to you and me, but we enjoy it now. I hope it has become habitual with us to abide with Jesus Christ. As morning breaks, we can frequently say, "When I awake, I am still with thee": and when the sun has gone down and we toss upon the bed unable to get to sleep, in the night watches our soul talks with Him whose eyes never slumber. Blessed is His name. This walking of Christ with His people is one of the daily privileges of the heir of heaven.

Another promise we have obtained is that of *divine covenanting*: "and I will be their God, and they shall be my people" (2 Cor. 6:16). God gives Himself to His people to be theirs, and they are His by the purchase of His own Son and the effectual conquest of the arm of His grace. He has chosen us for His inheritance and granted to us that He should become our portion and our inheritance. "I will be their God, and they shall be my people." Yes, God has entered into covenant relations with us, binding Himself to us by promise and oath. There are between us and our God bonds that cannot be snapped, links that can never be severed. Let us summon every faculty of our souls to praise His name.

In addition to all this, we have *divine adoption*: "[I] will be a Father unto you, and ye shall be my sons and daughters, saith the Lord Almighty" (2 Cor. 6:18). Is not this our blessed state? He loves us with a father's love, guides us with a father's care, protects us with a father's watchfulness, instructs us with a father's wisdom, bears with us with a father's patience, longs for us with a father's longing. We are His tender children, and He is our loving Parent. These are not things that are yet to come, like the second advent of our Lord in millennial splendor. They are promises that we have already obtained.

In the light of these blessings, how unspeakably great is the dignity of a Christian! Before we understood it, how we thirsted for it! We thought, when under conviction of sin, could we dare hope to be among God's people, it would be enough joy for us if we never had an earthly joy besides. I am afraid that since these blessings have become ours, we have not prized them as we should. Perhaps because of this we are sometimes brought into the prison of doubt, and our faith fails us. Just as we do not know the value of health till we are sick, so do we not value some of these blessed privileges until we have to walk in the dark and sigh and cry after unbroken fellowship amidst intermittent snatches of sweet assurance. May the Lord help His people to know the value of these heavenly realities that, in an abiding sense of their calling and their standing, they may act in a way that is worthy of such great dignities!

Now you perceive that it is necessary for us to get a good picture of the possessions of the Christian, because it is from these that Paul draws his argument, "Having therefore these promises." He uses, not the logic of the law or the logic of threatening, but the logic of love: "We have these mercies; we are so unspeakably favored; we are living in the daily enjoyment of divine indwelling, divine communion, divine covenanting, and divine adoption; therefore"—Paul takes a step forward by saying—"let us cleanse ourselves from all filthiness of the flesh and spirit." It is clear, then, that the doctrines of grace, redolent as they are of the privileges of the Christian, do not logically and spontaneously lead to licentiousness, as some have profanely said, but they naturally and reasonably lead to holiness of life. The fact that we are absolutely and unconditionally saved by God's grace, that our standing is secured, that we have become the children of God, is not an incentive to careless walking and to unholy living. Such an argument is the weak invention of the father of lies, for Satan is wont to palm off his offspring with a plausible appearance. But the argument is to gratitude in the heart and obedience in the life. What is obedience to God but holiness? True obedience would be holiness in perfection.

The Christian Labors to Be Rid of Obnoxious Evils

"Let us cleanse ourselves," says the apostle. What then? Do God's blood-bought, quickened people need cleansing? Are they such by nature that they must be cleansed? Ah, yes, every one of them, even the Apostle Paul himself! Where will you find a warmer spirit, a more zealous heart, a more consecrated man than the Apostle Paul? And yet *he* says, "Let us cleanse ourselves." I suppose that the nearer we get to heaven, the more conscious we shall be of our imperfections. The more light we get, the more we discover our own darkness. That which is scarcely accounted sin by some men will be a grievous defilement to a tender conscience. It is not that we are greater sinners as we grow older but that we have a finer sensibility of sin, and we now see sin where we once winked at it in the days of our ignorance. If it is to the holiest and most eminent of the people of God, how much more is it to us, common saints, who hardly feel worthy to be called saints at all, only that we trust we are washed in the precious blood and are saved through the righteousness of Jesus Christ. "Let *us* cleanse ourselves."

How pointedly the apostle puts it! I want you to notice the points. The work is *personal*. "Let us cleanse *ourselves*." It is more in accordance with our tastes to cleanse other people and attempt a moral reformation among our neighbors. It is easy to find out others' faults and to bring the whole force of our mind to bear against them. It is delightful to expose vice and lampoon the follies of the age, adding a dash of wit to enliven it, or to preach virtue, with a little of the sugar of scandal to sweeten a painful tale. It highly gratifies some people when they can find a fault with some highly respected person. That is their forte, the strength of their genius, pulling to pieces what they could not put together and attempting to raise themselves by lowering others. But notice, the apostle says, "Let us cleanse ourselves." Oh, that we would all look at home! Oh, that we did more indoor work in this department! Our first business is to "cleanse ourselves." It is all very well to drag the church of God up to the altar like some bleeding victim, and there to stab her with the sharpest knife of our criticism and to say that she is not this and she is not that. One might rather ask, "How far do I help to make her what she is? If she is degenerate, how far is that degeneracy consequent upon my having fallen from the high standing that I should have occupied?" We shall all have contributed our quota to the reform of the church when we are ourselves reformed. There can be no better way of promoting general holiness than by increasing in personal holiness.

Activity is needed, however, in discharging this personal duty. "Let us cleanse ourselves." It implies that the Christian, while he is acted upon by divine influence and cleansed by the Holy Spirit, is also an active agent of his own sanctification. He is not like the vessels and the pots of which the apostle speaks that were cleansed under the law. Man is a free agent, and the holiness that God works in him is not the pretended holiness of candlesticks and altars, but it is the holiness of a responsible being. It is a holiness that is not forced upon him, but one that his whole soul gives consent unto. He purges himself. Depend upon it, you and I do not grow holy by going to sleep. The Christian is developed by actively seeking growth, earnestly striving after holiness, and resolutely endeavoring to obtain it.

The utmost of our activity should be put forth in cleansing ourselves. Your bad temper will not be overcome by saying, "Well, you know I cannot help it." But you *must* help it; you must, if you are a believer. You have no more right to shake hands with a bad temper than you have to fraternize with the devil. You have got to overcome it, and in the name of God you must. Or if you happen to be lazy, you must not say, "Ah, well, you know, I am naturally so." Yes, what you are naturally we know: you are naturally as bad as you can be. But surely that is not the point. We are concerned with what you are to become by divine grace. Albeit sanctification is the work of the Holy Spirit, yet it is equally true that the Holy Spirit makes us active agents in our own sanctification. In the first work of regeneration, doubtless the soul is passive because it is dead, and the dead cannot contribute to their own quickening; but, being made alive, He "worketh in you both to will and to do of his good pleasure" (Phil. 2:13). God's good pleasure is answered by us when we are constrained to will and to do; hence the apostle's argument, "Work out your own salvation with fear and trembling. For it is God which worketh in you" (Phil. 2:12–13). He works it in, you work it out; you have to bring out in the outward life what He works in the inner springs of your spiritual being. You are to work it out because He works it in. Sin is to be driven out of us as the Canaanites were driven out of Canaan by the edge of the sword. Jericho's walls will come down, but not without being surrounded for seven days. Weary may be your march, but march you must if you would conquer. How does the apostle put it? "We wrestle not against flesh and blood" (Eph. 6:12), and so on; but he represents the conquest as being a conquest gained by wrestling. He declares that he had to fight with his old nature, and the conflict was stern. Although saved by grace, gracious souls make marvelous efforts— efforts beyond their natural powers—to enter into a state of rest from sin.

Nor must we stop short of *universality* in our purgings: "Let us purge ourselves *from all filthiness*." Your eye must not spare, your heart must not pity, one pet sin. Most people would willingly be holy if it were not for one particular sin that they vainly flatter themselves to be harmless. "From all filthiness let us cleanse ourselves." O Christian, you may very well doubt your right to that name unless all sin is obnoxious to you! You have no right to say, "I will give up pride and vanity," if you excuse yourself for being covetous. If covetousness is the leak in your vessel, it will sink it as surely as pride. If neither pride nor covetousness should be there, yet if you have an unforgiving temper and cannot be heartily reconciled to those who offend you, you shall just as soon prove yourself to be reprobate that way as by any other.

It must be an interesting sight to see the father of a Jewish family purging out the leaven before the Passover. He lights a candle, goes to the cupboard where the bread is kept, and takes care that every bit is put away. He then has every cupboard unlocked and rummages with a brush in his hand, and with a candle, too, to see lest there should be even a crumb of leaven, for he cannot keep the Passover if there is a crumb of leaven in the house. Such should be our earnest searching after all filthiness, to get it all out. Search as best we may, I am afraid something will still be left. There will be some beloved idol hidden away somewhere in the recesses of the mind. The heart will cling to its idols in such a style that we cannot find them all out at one investigation. They must be searched after, and we must be prepared to tear each from their throne. The apostle shows *the thoroughness of this work* by saying, "from *all filthiness of the flesh and spirit.*" "Filthiness of the flesh." We may reckon this to include all those outward sins so well known and so easily distinguishable, those degrading sins that even morality condemns. Possibly, although you may guard yourself against these, yet you will be in danger from the next class, namely, sins of the spirit. Sins of the spirit are full of that spawn that, when matured, issues in shameful delinquencies. If you can cleanse yourself from these, you will save yourself from dangers you little know. The outward life will be right enough when the inward life is right. I wish we were more concerned about cleansing ourselves from the filthiness of the spirit.

I am inclined to think that some people heedlessly pollute their spirits. I mean that they do it willfully. I am not sure that when there is a divorce case in the papers, I have any business to read it. Yet a great many Christian people, who often pray to be delivered from temptation, take pretty good care that they master all its details. When there is a bad story afloat about anyone, I do not know that I should listen to it. Yet that curiosity of ours often tempts the devil to tempt us. If there is a dirty puddle of water, I do not know that I am bound to take a drink of it. We may all do a great deal of that kind of thing. And nowadays, when the press ventilates everything and publishes it all over the world, I am sure that Christians do pollute their spirits a great deal more than they have any occasion to do. And besides that, we can turn over a sin in our mind till we become so accustomed to it that we do not think it is a sin. I know that some Christians have managed at last to cozen their conscience into the idea that what they do is not sin in them but would be sin in other people. Ah, dear friend, this will not do! "Let us cleanse ourselves from all filthiness of the flesh and spirit."

The drift of the argument is this—if God dwells in us, let us make the house clean for so pure a God. What! Indwelling Deity and unclean lusts? Indwelling Godhead and yet a spirit defiled with evil thoughts? God forbid! Let us cry out aloud to the Most High, that in this thing we may be cleansed, that the temple may be fit for the habitation of the Master. What! Does God walk in us and hold communion with us, and shall we let Belial come in? What fellowship can we have with Christ? Shall we give ourselves up to be the servants of Mammon, when God has become our Friend and Companion? It must not be! Divine indwelling and divine communion both require from us personal holiness. Has the Lord entered into a covenant with us that we shall be His people? Then does not this involve a call upon us to live in godliness like His people? Favored and privileged above other men to be a peculiar people, separated unto God's own self, shall there be nothing peculiar about our lives? Shall we not be zealous for good works?

Divinely adopted into the family of the Most High, made heirs of God and joint heirs with Jesus Christ, what need is there of further argument to constrain us to holiness? You see the "therefore." It is just this, because we have attained to such choice and special privileges, "therefore"—for this reason—"let us cleanse ourselves."

Aiming at a Most Exalted Position

"Perfecting holiness" describes the aim of the Christian life. *"But can a Christian be perfect in this life?"* When this question was put to me, I answered, "No." "Well, is the Christian perfect when he gets to heaven?" "Yes." "Well, then, he was perfect when he died, was he not?" I thought he must be. I do not understand any change taking place between the moment of departure from this world and the moment of entrance into heaven. "Very well!" was the answer. "But he was in the flesh, then, you know." The question thus turned on being in the flesh, and the answer is obvious. The flesh is inherently sinful, and all its carnal desires are at enmity against God. Perfection at present does not aim at regenerating the old nature; such perfection will be effected at the resurrection of the just. But as many as are perfect must control and keep the flesh and its desires completely under dominion (Gal. 5:24). That is our present duty. If the death of the body looses us from sin, the mortification of our members that are upon the earth must be our continual aim till we are delivered from the bondage of corruption.

An illustration may explain my meaning. I can imagine a room in your house being perfectly clean, but I cannot imagine its being kept perfectly clean unless the process by which it was first cleansed is frequently repeated. Whether that room is in constant use or whether it is shut up, it will require to be swept and dusted every day or it will not be perfectly clean very long.

I recall hearing a man say that he had lived for six years without having sinned in either thought, word, or deed. It seemed to me that if he had known anything about his own heart, he would not have dared to speak thus confidently. Were it true of me, I think I should be like a man who had diamonds about him and dared not tell anybody for fear the mention of it should prompt someone to rob him of his treasure. I should keep it to myself. If such a priceless pearl as perfection can belong to any of the saints, and I were the happy possessor, I should be very jealous of it lest anyone should know it and seek to deprive me of it. No, no; I cannot believe that the flesh can be perfect, nor, consequently, that anyone can be perfect in this flesh. I cannot believe that we shall ever live to see people walking up and down in this world without sin. But I can believe that it is our duty to be perfect, that the law of God means perfection, and that the law as it is in Christ is binding on the Christian. It is not, as in the hands of Moses, armed with power to justify or to condemn him, for he is not under the law but under grace; but it is binding upon him as it is in the hands of Christ. The law, as it is in the hands of Christ, is just as glorious, just as perfect, just as complete, as when it was in the hands of Moses. Christ did not come to destroy the law or to cast it down, but to establish it; and therefore, notwithstanding every point where I fall short of perfection as a creature, I am complete in Christ Jesus. That which Christ requires of me is that I should be perfect.

That I can understand, and the next thing I should know is that *for such perfection I should pray*. I should not pray for anything short of that. Our prayer must be, "Lord, put away all sin; deliver me from it altogether." And God would not teach you to pray for what He did not mean to give. Your perfection is God's design, for He has chosen you to be conformed to the image of His Son. And what is that? Surely the image of His Son is perfection. There were no faults in the Lord Jesus Christ. We are to be made like Him; and as this is the work and design of grace, then perfection is the center of the target at which God's grace is always aiming. All that He works in us is with this great ultimate end and aim of sanctifying us wholly—spirit, soul, and body; and that He may release us from sin and make us perfect even as our Father who is in heaven is perfect. Oh, when will it be? When will it be? The very thought of it makes me feel as if I could sing. What a joy it will be to be just like Him, to have no more corruption of the flesh and no more incitements to sin to destroy the soul's delight and pleasure in her God! May the Lord hasten on the day! "Perfecting holiness."

When a young artist begins to work, he studies the most perfect models he can find. He studies Raphael; he wants to see what Michelangelo could do. "Oh!" says one. "What are you trying to paint? Are you trying to be a Raphael? Will you ever paint like Michelangelo?" Never. But the only possibility of his being a good artist is his taking perfect models. So with you. Your model is the perfect Savior, and this is to be what you are to aim at every day: "perfecting holiness." And for all you may say, "Ah! I shall never come up to that; many failures have proved to me that I shall not reach it." Yet you will do better with that as your ambition than you could have done if you had selected some imperfect model and said, "Well, if I am as good as that man, that will suit me." Nothing but perfection must content you. Press forward toward it, and God speed you in the race!

Prompted by the Most Sacred of Motives

"Perfecting holiness *in the fear of God.*" An abiding sense of God's presence, a perpetual feeling of our obligations to our Creator, produces a reverent fear of God—not the slavish, servile fear that brings torment, but the fear that bows the tall archangel in adoration before the throne, the fear that makes the cherub veil his face with his wings while he adores the Lord. Such a constant fear as this is the mainspring of Christian holiness. Not the fear of man, though many people are kept moral by that; not the fear of some Christian man whom you respect, lest he should upbraid you for falling short. No, your great motive is to be the fear of God. Not the fear of the public eye, which is such a fickle thing. Have you noticed that the very thing that the world calls "bad and shameful," if it does not succeed, would be thought clever and to be admired, if it succeeded. The world only appreciates success; that is the measure of the world's morality. The true Christian has a higher system of ethics. He perfects holiness in the fear of God; and if he should be successful and the world says, "Well done! Well done!" yet, if he felt he had done a wrong thing or an unholy thing, his conscience would prick him. He would be as uneasy as though everyone pointed the finger of scorn at him. I think he would be as restless as Zaccheus was until he had made a just disposition of his unholy gains.

I cannot speak to you as I wish. But were the hour of my departure come, were I allowed but to utter one sentence and then I must die, I would say to you, "Be holy!" And if you will not be holy, do us the favor to lay down your profession of faith. If you *will* have your sins and go to hell, you can do it so much better outside the church than you can inside. I cannot see why you must live as Christ's enemy and yet profess to be His friend. Get out of the church, you that are hypocrites! Why should you come unless you intend to be a true follower of the Crucified? If you love the world, why do you pretend to love the church? Judas, Judas, go sell somebody else; why do you need to sell Christ and to be the son of perdition? You who are unholy, you who cheat in business, you who can lie in your daily lives, there is room enough for you outside of God's church. Why do you need to come with your filthiness where you are not asked to come? The Word of God calls His saints to come out and be separate from such.

Be holy, be holy, be holy! You who are workers, be holy in the workplace. You who are employers, show holiness among your workers. Mothers and fathers, let your children see your godliness. Children, may the Holy Spirit make you the holiest of children, like the holy child Jesus! And may it be a point with each of us that if we live, we live unto Christ, so that when we die, we may be found in Him, made ready to be partakers of the inheritance of the saints in light.

This wonderful life, resulting in the blended personality of the believer and the Son of God, is a true life. This is expressed in the text, "Nevertheless I live"—yes, live as I never lived before. When the apostle declares himself to be dead to the world, he would not have us imagine that he was dead in the highest and best sense. No, he lived with a new force and vigor of life. It seemed to me that when I came to know Christ, I was just like a butterfly newly burst from the cocoon. I then began really to live. When a soul is startled by the thunder claps of conviction and afterwards receives pardon in Christ, it begins to live. The worldling says he wants to see life, and therefore plunges into sin! Fool that he is, he peers into the sepulcher to discover immortality. The man who truly lives is the believer. Shall I become less active because I am a Christian? God forbid! Should I become less industrious, find fewer opportunities for the manifestation of my natural and spiritual energies? God forbid! If ever a man should be like a sword too sharp for the scabbard, with an edge that cannot be dulled, it should be the Christian. He should be like flames of fire burning his way. Live while you live. Let there be no frittering away of time. Live so as to demonstrate that you possess the noblest form of life.

Chapter Four

Crucified with Christ

I am crucified with Christ: nevertheless I live; yet not I, but Christ liveth in me: and the life which I now live in the flesh I live by the faith of the Son of God, who loved me, and gave himself for me—
Galatians 2:20.

IN GREAT RANGES OF MOUNTAINS there are lofty peaks that pierce the clouds, but on the other hand, there are lower parts of the range that are crossed by travelers, becoming national highways that afford passages for commerce from country to country. My text rises before my contemplation like a lofty range of mountains, a very Andes for elevation. I shall not attempt to climb the summits of its sublimity, but I shall, to the best of my ability, conduct you over one or two practical truths that may be helpful to you.

The Personality of the Christian Faith

How many personal pronouns of the first person are there in this verse? Are there not as many as eight? The verse swarms with *I* and *me*. The text does not mention someone else or a third party far away. The apostle speaks of himself, his own inner life, his own spiritual death, the love of Christ to *him*, and the great sacrifice that Christ made for *him*. "Who loved *me*, and gave himself for *me*." This is instructive, for it is a distinguishing mark of Christianity that it brings out a person's individuality. It does not make us selfish. On the contrary, it cures us of that evil, but still it does manifest in us a selfhood by which we become conscious of our personal individuality in a profound sense.

In the nocturnal heavens there had long been observed bright masses of light that the astronomers called "nebulae." The astronomers supposed them to be stores of unfashioned chaotic matter, until the telescope of Herschell resolved them into distinct stars. What the telescope did for stars, the religion of Christ, when received into the heart, does for men. Men tend to think of themselves as mixed up with the race or absorbed in universal manhood. They have a very indistinct idea of their separate obligations to God and their personal relations to His government. But the gospel, like a telescope, brings a man out of himself, makes him see himself as a separate existence, and compels him to meditate upon his own sin, his own salvation, and his own personal doom unless saved by grace. In the broad road there are so many travelers that as one takes a bird's-eye view of it, it appears to be filled with a vast mob of people moving on without order. But in the straight and narrow way that leads to life eternal, every traveler is distinct. Having to go against the general current of the times, the believer is an individual upon whom observant eyes are fixed. He is a distinct individual, both to himself and to the rest of his kind.

You will readily see how the religion of Jesus Christ brings out a person's individuality *in its very dawn;* it reveals to him his own personal sin and consequent danger. You know nothing about conversion if you merely believe in human depravity and human ruin but have never felt that *you* are depraved and that *you yourself* are ruined. Over and above all the general woes of the race, there will be one particular woe of your own if you have been convinced of sin by the Holy Spirit. You will feel as if the arrows of God were mainly aimed at you and as if the curses of the law would surely fall upon you if upon none else. Certainly, you know nothing about salvation unless you have *personally looked with your own eye to Jesus Christ.* There must be a personal reception of the Lord Jesus into the arms of your faith and into the bosom of your love. If you have not trusted in the Crucified while standing alone in contemplation at the foot of the cross, you have not believed unto life eternal.

In consequence of a separate personal faith, the believer enjoys *a personal peace.* He feels that if the whole world were at war, he would still find rest in Christ—that rest being particularly his own, independent of others. He may talk of that peace to others, but he cannot communicate it; others cannot give it to him, nor can they take it from him. Wherever the Christian faith is truly in the soul, it soon leads to *a personal consecration* to God. The man comes to the altar of Christ and cries, "Here I am, O most glorious Lord; I feel it is my reasonable service to give spirit, soul, and body to You. Let others do as they will; as for me and my house, we will serve the Lord." The renewed man feels that the work of others does not excuse him from service, and the lukewarmness of the church cannot be an excuse for his own indifference. He stands out against error, if need be, as a lone protestor, like Athanasius, crying, "I, Athanasius, against the whole world." Or he works for God in the building up of Jerusalem, like Nehemiah, being content to work alone if others will not assist him. He has discovered himself to have been personally lost as well as saved, and now his prayer is, "Lord, show me what You would have *me* do. Here am *I*, send *me.*" I believe that in proportion as our godliness is definitely in the first person singular, it will be strong and vigorous.

I believe, moreover, that in proportion as we fully realize our personal responsibility to God, we shall be likely to fulfill it. If we have not really understood it, we are likely to dream of work for God by proxy, to pay a priest or the minister to be useful for us, acting as if we could shift our responsibility from our own shoulders to the back of a church. From its dawn up to its noonday glory, the personality of true godliness is most observable. All the teaching of our holy faith bears in this direction. We preach personal election, personal calling, personal regeneration, personal perseverance, personal holiness, and we know nothing of any work of grace that is not personal to the professor of it. There is no doctrine in Scripture that teaches that one man can be saved by the godliness of another, except in the one case of the sponsorship of the Lord Jesus Christ. I find no human being placed in the role of another so as to be able to take another's burden of sin or perform another's duty. I do find that we are to bear one another's burden and give an account for ourself before God. It is so simple a truth that when I make the statement, you perhaps wonder that I should repeat it so often; but simple as it is, it is constantly being forgotten. How many church members shelter themselves behind the vigorous action of the entire community! The church is growing, the church opens schools, the church is active in outreach to the community, and so the church member flatters himself that he is doing something, whereas that person may not have—either by his contributions, prayers, or personal teachings—done anything at all. To such persons, I beseech you, shake yourself from the dust. Never attempt to appropriate other men's labors. Before your own Master you shall stand or fall upon your own individual service or neglect, and if you do not bring forth fruit yourself, all the fruit upon the other branches shall not avail for you. "Every tree that bringeth not forth good fruit is hewn down, and cast into the fire" (Matt. 7:19). "Every branch in me that beareth not fruit he taketh away" (John 15:2).

It is common also for persons to shelter themselves behind a missionary work. A small annual contribution has often been a cloak for gross indifference to holy discipleship. Somebody else is paid to be a missionary and to do the mission work: is this the Lord's way? Is this the path of obedience? Does not our Lord say to us, "As my Father hath sent me, even so send I you" (John 20:21)? The Father did not send Christ that He might procure a proxy and be a nominal Redeemer, but Jesus gave Himself for us in personal service and sacrifice: even so does Jesus send us forth to suffer and to serve. It is good to support the minister as well as the missionary that they may have time to give to needful work. But remember, when all the fulltime Christian workers have done all that is possible, they cannot exonerate you from your own peculiar calling, and however large your contributions to assist others to serve the Master, they cannot discharge on your behalf one single particle of what was due from you personally to your Lord. You must stand forth in your own character and remember that before God you must be estimated by what *you* have felt, what *you* have known, what *you* have learned, and what *you* have done.

The worst form of lie is when people imagine that family piety and national religion can ever be available in lieu of individual repentance and faith. Absurd as it may seem, yet a very common thing is for people to say, "Oh, yes! We are all Christians—of course, we are all Christians—every Englishman is a Christian." Is a rat a horse because it lives in a stable? That is just as good reasoning. A man must be born again or he is no child of God. A man must have a living faith in Jesus Christ or else he is no Christian.

Others say, "My mother and father always professed such a religion, therefore I am bound to do the same." Glorious reasoning, fit for idiots most surely! I have known people impressed by the gospel who have nevertheless clung to the false hopes of superstition or human merit and have excused themselves by saying, "You see, I have always been brought up to it." Does a man think that because his mother was poor and his father a pauper, that he himself must remain a beggar? No. But if I have beheld the light of the truth of Jesus Christ, let me follow it and not be drawn aside by the idea that hereditary superstition is any the less dangerous or erroneous because a dozen generations have been deluded by it. You must appear before God on your own feet, and neither mother nor father can stand in your place. Seek eternal life for yourself. Lift up your eyes to Christ's cross for yourself and let it be your own earnest endeavor that you may be able to say, "He loved *me* and gave himself for *me*."

We all come alone as pilgrims into this world to traverse a path that only our own feet can tread. To a great extent we go through the world alone, for all our companions are but vessels sailing with us side by side, vessels distinct and bearing each one its own flag. Into the depths of our heart no man can dive. There are cabinets in the chamber of the soul that no man can open but the individual himself. We must die alone—friends may surround the bed, but the departing spirit must take its flight by itself. We shall hear no tramp of thousands as we descend into the dark river; we shall be solitary travelers into the unknown land. We expect to stand before the judgment seat of Christ in the midst of a great assembly, but still to be judged as if no other man were there. If all that multitude is condemned and we are in Christ, we shall be saved; and if they should all be saved and we are found lacking, we shall be cast away. In the balances we shall each be placed alone. There is a crucible for every ingot of gold, a furnace for every bar of silver. In the resurrection every person shall receive his own body. There shall be an individuality about the body that shall be raised in that day of wonders, an individuality most marked and manifest. If I am condemned at the last, no man can be damned for my spirit. No soul can enter the chambers of fire on my behalf, to endure for me the unutterable anguish. And, blessed hope, if I am saved, it will be *I* who shall see the King in His beauty: "mine eyes shall behold, and not another" (Job 19:27). The joys of heaven shall not be proxy joys but will be the personal enjoyments of those who have had personal union with Christ. Let us not play the fool with eternal things, but let us desire to have a personal interest in Christ, and then let us aspire to give to Him, who deserves it so well, our personal service, rendering spirit, soul, and body to His cause.

The Interweaving of Our Personality with That of Jesus Christ

Read the text again, "I am crucified with Christ; nevertheless I live; yet not I, but Christ liveth in me: and the life which I now live in the flesh I live by the faith of the Son of God, who loved me, and gave himself for me." Here is the redeemed man, but here is the Son of God quite as conspicuously, and the two personalities are singularly interwoven. I picture two trees before me. They are distinct plants growing side by side, but as I follow them downward, I observe that the roots are so interlaced and intertwisted that no one can trace the separate trees. Such are Christ and the believer. Imagine with me a vine. Yonder is a branch, distinct and perfect as a branch. It is not to be mistaken for any other. It is a branch—a whole and perfect branch—yet how perfectly it is joined to the stem and how completely its individuality is merged in the one vine of which it is a member! So it is with the believer in Christ.

There is one parent man who threw his shadow across our path and from whose influence we could never escape. From all other men we might have struggled away and claimed to be separate, but this man was part of ourselves, and we part of him—Adam the first, in his fallen state. We are fallen with Adam and broken in pieces in his ruin. And now, glory be to God, as the shadow of the first man has been uplifted from us, there appears a second man, the Lord from heaven. Across our path there falls the light of His glory and His excellence, from which also we who have believed in Him cannot escape. In the light of that Man, the second Adam, the heavenly federal Head of all His people—in His light we do rejoice. Interwoven with our history and personality is the history and personality of the Man Christ Jesus, and we are forever one with Him.

Observe the points of contact. First Paul says, *I am crucified with Christ.* What does he intend? He means a great many more things than I can tell you, but he certainly means this: he believed in the representation of Christ on the cross. He held that when Jesus Christ hung upon the tree, He did not hang there as a private person but as the representative of all His chosen people. The Lord Jesus Christ acted in what He did as a great public representative person, and the dying of Jesus Christ upon the tree was the virtual dying of all His people. *I am crucified with Christ.* The apostle to the Gentiles delighted to think that as one of Christ's chosen people, he died upon the tree in Christ. He did more than believe this doctrinally, however. He accepted it confidently, resting his hope upon it. He believed that by virtue of Jesus Christ's death, he had himself paid the law its due, satisfied divine justice, and found reconciliation with God.

What a blessed thing it is when the soul can, as it were, stretch itself upon the cross of Christ and feel, "I am dead; the law has killed me, cursed me, slain me, and I am therefore free from its power, because in my Surety I have borne the curse, and in the person of my Substitute the whole that the law could do, by way of condemnation, has been executed upon me, for I am crucified with Christ." How blessed it is when the cross of Christ is laid upon us! How it gives us life! Union with the suffering, bleeding Savior and faith in the merit of the Redeemer are soul-cheering things. Oh, for more enjoyment of them!

Paul meant even more than this. He not only believed in Christ's death and trusted in it but also actually felt its power in himself in causing the crucifixion of his old corrupt nature. If you conceive of yourself as a man executed, you at once perceive that, being executed by the law, the law has no further claim upon you. You resolve, moreover, that having once proven the curse of sin by the sentence passed upon you, you will not fall into that same offense again, but henceforth, being miraculously delivered from the death into which the law brought you, you will live in newness of life. You must feel so if you feel rightly. Thus did Paul view himself as a criminal upon whom the sentence of the law had been fulfilled. When he saw the pleasures of sin, he said, "I cannot enjoy these: I am dead to them. I once had a life in which these were very sweet to me, but I have been crucified with Christ. Consequently, as a dead man can have no delight in the joys that once were delights to him, so neither can I."

When Paul looked upon the carnal things of the world, he said, "I once allowed these things to reign over me. What shall I eat? What shall I drink? How shall I be clothed? These were a trinity of questions of the utmost importance. They are of no importance now, because I am dead to these things. I cast my care upon God with regard to them. They are not my life. I am crucified to them." If any passion, if any motive, if any design should come into our mind—short of the cross of Christ—we should exclaim, "God forbid that I should glory in any of these things; I am a dead man. Come, world, with all your witchery; come, pleasure, with all your charms; come, wealth, with all your temptations; come, all you tempters that have seduced so many. What can you do with a crucified person? How can you tempt one who is dead to you?" It is a blessed state of mind when a man can feel that through having received Christ he is to this world as one who is utterly dead. Neither does he yield his strength to its purposes, nor his soul to its customs, nor his judgment to its maxims, nor his heart to its affections, for he is a crucified man through Jesus Christ. The world is crucified to him, and he to the world. That is what the apostle meant.

Notice next another point of contact. He says, *Nevertheless, I live,* but then he corrects himself, *yet not I, but Christ liveth in me.* You have seen the dead side of a believer: he is deaf and dumb and blind and without feeling to the sinful world, yet he adds, *Nevertheless I live.* He explains what his life is—his life is produced in him by virtue of Christ's being in him and his being in Christ. Jesus is the source of the Christian's life. The sap in the vine lives even in the smallest of the tendrils. So in every believer. Though the Christian may be insignificant and possess little grace, yet still, if he is truly a believer, Jesus lives in him. The life that keeps his faith, his hope, his love still in existence comes from Jesus Christ and from Him alone. We should cease to be living saints if we did not daily receive grace from our covenant Head. As the strength of our life comes from the Son of God, so is He the ruler and moving power within us.

How can he be a Christian who is ruled by anything but Christ? If you call Christ "Master and Lord," you must be His servant. Nor can you yield obedience to any rival power, for no man can serve two masters. There must be a master-spirit in the heart, and unless Jesus Christ is such a master-spirit to us, we are not saved at all. The life of the Christian is a life that springs from Christ, and it is controlled by His will. Has the life that you have lived been Christ's living in you? Have you been like a book printed in plain letters in which men might read a new edition of the life of Jesus Christ? A Christian should be a living photograph of the Lord Jesus, a striking likeness of his Lord. When men look at a believer, they should see not only what the Christian is but also what the Christian's Master is, for the Christian should be like his Master. Do you ever sense that within your soul Christ looks out through your eyes, regarding poor sinners and considering how you may help them? Do you sense that Christ throbs in your heart, feeling for the perishing, trembling for those who will not tremble for themselves? Do you ever feel Christ opening your hands in liberal charity to help those who cannot help themselves? Have you ever felt that something more than yourself was in you, a spirit that sometimes struggles with yourself and holds it by the throat and threatens to destroy its sinful selfishness—a noble spirit that puts its foot upon the neck of covetousness, a brave spirit that dashes to the ground your pride, an active fervent spirit that burns up your laziness? Have you never felt this? Truly we who live unto God feel the life of God within and desire to be more and more subdued under the dominant spirit of Christ, that our lives may be a palace for the Well-beloved. That is another point of contact.

Further on, the apostle says, *The life which I now live in the flesh I live by the faith of the Son of God.* Every moment of the Christian life is to be a life of faith. We make a mistake when we try to walk by feeling or by sight. I dreamed the other night while musing upon the life of the believer that I was passing along a road that a divine call had appointed for me. The ordained pathway that I was called to travel was amid thick darkness, unmingled with a ray of light. As I stood in the awful gloom, unable to perceive a single inch before me, I heard a voice that said, "Let your feet go straight on. Fear not, but advance in the name of God." So on I went, putting down foot after foot with trembling. After a little while, the path through the darkness became easy and smooth. Just then I perceived that the path turned, and it was of no use my attempting to proceed as I had before. The way was tortuous, and the road was rough and stony; but I remembered what was said, that I was to advance as I could, and so on I went. Then there came another twist, and yet another, and another, and another, and I wondered why, till I understood that if the path ever remained long the same, I would grow accustomed to it and so begin to walk by feeling. I learned that the whole of the way would constantly be such as to compel me to depend upon the guiding voice, exercising faith in the unseen One who had called me.

Suddenly it appeared to me as though there was nothing beneath my foot when I put it down, yet I thrust it out into the darkness in confident daring, and lo, a firm step was reached, and another, and another, as I walked down a staircase that descended deep, down, down, down. Onward I passed, not seeing an inch before me, but believing that all was well, although I could hear around me the dash of falling men and women who had walked by the light of their own lanterns and missed their foothold. I heard the cries and shrieks of men as they fell from this dreadful staircase. But I was commanded to go right on, and I went straight on, resolved to be obedient even if the way should descend into the nethermost hell. By and by the dreadful ladder was ended, and I found a solid rock beneath my feet and walked straight ahead upon a paved causeway with a railing on either hand. I understood this to be the experience that I had gained, that now could guide and help me, and I leaned on this railing and walked on confidently until my causeway ended and my feet sank in the mire. As for my other comforts, I groped for them, but they were gone, for still I was to know that I must go in dependence upon my unseen Friend. I knew that the road would always be such that no experience could serve me instead of dependence upon God. Forward I plunged through mire and filth and suffocating smoke and a smell as of death-damp, for it was *the* way that I had been commanded to walk.

Again the pathway changed, though all was midnight still. Up went the path, and up and up and up, with nothing upon which I could lean. Wearily I ascended innumerable stairs, not one of which I could see, although the very thought of their height might make the brain reel. Then suddenly my pathway burst into light, as I woke from my reverie. When I looked down upon it, I saw it all to be safe, but such a road that if I had seen it I never could have walked it. It was only in the darkness that I could have performed my mysterious journey, only in childlike confidence upon the Lord. The Lord will guide us if we are willing to do just as He tells us. Lean upon Him, then. I have painted a poor picture, but still one that if you can realize it, will be grand to look upon. To walk straight on, believing in Christ every moment, believing your sins are forgiven even when you see their blackness, believing that you are safe when you seem in the utmost danger, believing that you are glorified with Christ when you feel as if you were cast out from God's presence—this is the life of faith.

Furthermore, Paul notes other points of unity. *Who loved me.* Blessed be God, before the mountains lifted up their snow-crowned heads to the clouds, Christ had set His heart upon us. His "delights were with the sons of men" (Prov. 8:31). In His "book all [his] members were written, which in continuance were fashioned, when as yet there was none of them" (Ps. 139:16). Believer, get a hold of the precious truth that Christ loved you eternally—the all-glorious Son of God chose you and espoused you unto Himself, that you might be His bride throughout eternity. Here is a blessed union indeed.

Observe the next, *and gave himself for me*—not only gave all that He had, but gave Himself; not merely laid aside His glory and His splendor and His life, but yielded up His very self. O heir of heaven, Jesus is yours at this moment. Having given Himself once for you upon the tree to put your sin away, at this moment He gives Himself to you to be your life, your crown, your joy, your portion, your all in all. You have found out yourself to be a separate personality and individual, but that personality is linked with the person of Christ Jesus, so that you are in Christ and Christ is in you. By a blessed indissoluble union you are knit together forever and ever.

The Life That Results from This Blended Personality

When a man finds and knows himself to be linked with Christ, his life is altogether *a new life*. I gather that from the expression, "I am crucified, nevertheless I live." Crucified, then dead; crucified, then the old life is put away—whatever life a crucified man has must be new life. So is it with you. Upon your old life, believer, a sentence of death has been pronounced. The carnal mind, which is enmity against God (Rom. 8:7), is doomed to die. You can say with Paul, "I die daily" (1 Cor. 15:31). Would to God the old nature were completely dead. But whatever you have of life was not given you until you came into union with Christ. It is a new thing, as new as though you had been actually dead and rotted in the grave and then had started up at the sound of the trumpet to live again. You have received a life from above, a life that the Holy Spirit wrought in you in regeneration. That which is born of the flesh is flesh, but your grace-life did not come from yourself: you have been born again from above.

Your life is *a very strange one*—"I am crucified, nevertheless I live." What a contradiction! The Christian's life is a matchless riddle. No worldling can comprehend it; even the believer himself cannot understand it. He knows it, but as to solving all its enigmas, he feels that to be an impossible task. Dead, yet alive; crucified with Christ, and yet at the same time risen with Christ in newness of life! Do not expect the world to understand you, Christian, it did not understand your Master. When your actions are misrepresented and your motives are ridiculed, do not be surprised. "If ye were of the world, the world would love his own: but because ye are not of the world, but I have chosen you out of the world, therefore the world hateth you" (John 15:19). If you belonged to the village, the dogs would not bark at you. If men could read you, they would not wonder. It is because you are written in celestial language that men cannot comprehend you and thus think you worthless. Your life is new; your life is strange.

This wonderful life, resulting in the blended personality of the believer and the Son of God, is *a true life*. This is expressed in the text, "Nevertheless I live"—yes, live as I never lived before. When the apostle declares himself to be dead to the world, he would not have us imagine that he was dead in the highest and best sense. No, he lived with a new force and vigor of life. It seemed to me that when I came to know Christ, I was just like a butterfly newly burst from the cocoon. I then began really to live. When a soul is startled by the thunder claps of conviction and afterwards receives pardon in Christ, it begins to live. The worldling says he wants to see life, and therefore plunges into sin! Fool that he is, he peers into the sepulcher to discover immortality. The man who truly lives is the believer. Shall I become less active because I am a Christian? God forbid! Should I become less industrious, find fewer opportunities for the manifestation of my natural and spiritual energies? God forbid! If ever a man should be like a sword too sharp for the scabbard, with an edge that cannot be dulled, it should be the Christian. He should be like flames of fire burning his way. Live while you live. Let there be no frittering away of time. Live so as to demonstrate that you possess the noblest form of life.

It is also clear that the new life that Christ brings to us is a life of *self-abnegation*, for Paul adds, "I live, yet not I." Lowliness of mind is part and parcel of godliness. He who can take any credit to himself knows not the spirit of our holy faith. The believer when he prays best says, "Yet not I, but the Spirit of God interceded in me." If he has won any souls to Christ, he says, "Yet not I; it was the gospel. The Lord Jesus worked in me mightily." Self-humiliation is the native spirit of the true-born child of God.

Further, the life that Christ works in us is a life of *one idea*. Is the believer's soul ruled by two things? No, he knows but one. "Christ liveth in me." One Lord and Master I serve. Do you live this way? Alas! I mourn that I live too much in the old life, and too little does Jesus live in me. But the Christian, if he should ever come to perfection—and God grant we each may come as near to it as possible even now—will find that the old "I live" is kept under and the new Christ-life reigns supreme. Christ must be the one thought, the one idea, the one master-thought in the believer's soul. When the healthy believer wakes in the morning, he inquires, "What can I do for Christ?" When he goes about his business, he asks, "How shall I serve my Lord in all my actions?" When he makes money, he questions himself, "How can I use my finances for Christ?" If he acquires education, the challenge is, "How can I spend my knowledge for Christ?"

To sum up much in little, the child of God has within him the *Christ-life*. But how shall I describe that? Christ's life on earth was the divine mingled with the human—such is the life of the Christian. There is something divine about it. It is born of a living, incorruptible seed, which abideth forever (1 Pet. 1:23). We are made partakers of the divine nature, having escaped the corruption that is in the world through lust, yet our life is thoroughly human life. The Christian is a man among men. In all that is manly he labors to excel, yet he is not as other men are, but wears a hidden nature that no mere worldling understands. Picture the life of Christ on earth, and that is what the life of God in us should be and will be in proportion as we are subject to the power of the Holy Spirit.

Notice again, keeping close to the text, that the life that God works in us is still *the life of a man*. "The life which I now live in the flesh," says the apostle. Religious people who run away from the world for fear that its temptations should overcome them, secluding themselves for the sake of greater holiness, are as excellent as soldiers who retreat to the camp for fear of being defeated. Of what service are such soldiers in the warfare of life? Christ did not come to make monks of us: He came to make *men* of us. He meant that we should learn how to *live in the flesh*. We are to give up neither business nor society, nor in any right sense are we to give up life. "The life I live in the flesh," says the apostle. Look at him busy at his tentmaking. What! An apostle making tents? What would we say to the Archbishop of Canterbury stitching away for his living? It is too low for a bishop certainly, but not too low for Paul. I do not think the apostle was ever more apostolic than when he picked up sticks. When Paul and his companions were shipwrecked at Melita, he set to work like other people to gather fuel for the fire (Acts 28:3). Even so, you and I must take our turn at the wheel. We must not think of keeping ourselves aloof from our fellowmen, as though we should be degraded by mingling with them. The salt of the earth should be well rubbed into the meat, and so the Christian should mingle with his fellowmen, seeking their good for edification. We are men, and whatever men may lawfully do, we do; wherever they may go, we may go. Our religion makes us neither more nor less than human, though it brings us into the family of God.

Yet the Christian life *is a life of faith.* "The life which I live in the flesh, I live by the faith of the Son of God." Faith is not a garment to be worn on Sundays. It is a working principle to be used in the barn and in the field, in the shop and in the business. It is a grace for the housewife and the servant. It is for the highest office of government and for the poorest workshop. I would have the believing cobbler mend shoes religiously and the tailor make garments by faith, and I would have every Christian buy and sell by faith. Whatever your work may be, faith is to be taken into your daily callings, and that is alone the truly living faith that will bear the practical test. You are not to stop at the shop door and say, "Farewell to Christianity till I finish my work for the day." That is hypocrisy. The genuine life of the Christian is the life that we live *in the flesh by the faith of the Son of God.*

To conclude: the life that comes out of the blended personality of the believer and Christ is a life of *perfect love.* "He gave himself for me." My question is, therefore, What can I do for Him? The new life is a life of *holy security,* for if Christ loved me, who can destroy me? It is a life of *holy wealth,* for if Christ gave His infinite self to me, what can I want? It is a life of *holy joy,* for if Christ is mine, I have a well of holy joy within my soul. It is *the life of heaven,* for if I have Christ, I have that which is the essence and soul of heaven.

If you have understood these truths, believer, take them into your home and live out the truth. Practice that which is practicable, feed upon that which is full of savor, rejoice in Christ Jesus that you are one with Him, and then, in your own proper person, go out and serve your Master with might and strength, and the Lord send you His abundant blessing.

Every man sees morally what he is himself. A man who is bad sees evil and is blind to good. The man who is partially like Christ has only a partial view of Christ. If your eye does not see inexpressible beauty in Him, it is your eye that is to blame, for He is altogether lovely. And when the eye of our inward nature shall come to see Jesus as He is, then we may depend upon it that we are like Him. It is the pure in heart who see God (Matt. 5:8) because God, the inexpressibly pure One, can be seen only by those who are themselves pure. When we shall be perfectly pure, we shall be able to understand Christ; and when we understand Christ, or see Him as He is, as we shall do at His appearing, then we shall be like Him—free from sin, full of consecration to God, pure and perfect. Today, He is Conqueror over sin and death and hell; He is superlative in His virtue and His holiness; He has conquered all the powers of evil; and one day we too shall put our foot on the old dragon's head, we too shall see sin crushed beneath us, and we shall come off ''more than conquerors through him that loved us'' (Rom. 8:37). This, then, is our hope, that we shall be like our Head when we shall see Him as He is.

Chapter Five

The Hope That Purifies

Beloved, now are we the sons of God, and it doth not yet appear what we shall be: but we know that when he shall appear, we shall be like him; for we shall see him as he is. And every man that hath this hope in him purifieth himself, even as he is pure—
1 John 3:2–3.

THE CHRISTIAN is a person who should be noted as someone who experiences a great deal of joy. "Beloved, now are we the sons of God"; and being God's sons, we cannot be altogether unhappy. A relationship to the ever-blessed God must bring with it a measure of joy. "Happy art thou, O Israel:" sang Moses, "who is like unto thee, O people saved by the LORD" (Deut. 33:29). Those who can be truly called the sons of God are a blessed people. Still, the main portion of the believer's inheritance lies not so much in what I have as what I shall have. "It doth not yet appear what we shall be." To the unbeliever, all that is to come is in darkness. He may expect to go from the shades of evening to the blackness of a midnight that shall never end; but for the Christian, "light is sown" (Ps. 97:11). He is in darkness now—the only darkness he shall ever know—and from the twilight of the morning he shall go on to the perfect day, a day whose sun shall never set. We have the eyes of hope given to us, and looking past the narrow stream of death and beyond that place where to carnal eyes hangs the curtain that shuts out the unseen, we behold the glory that is yet to be revealed, and we are blessed with the joys of hope. Let every Christian, therefore, when at any time he is downcast about the things of the present, refresh his soul with the thought of the future.

I know that some of us have frequently been cheered and comforted by seeing how kindly God has dealt with us in bringing us up out of the pit of our past. Now we shall get further consolation by seeing what is to become of us in the future yet to be revealed. But still, my object at this time will not be to impart consolation so much as to stimulate holiness. Our text is a very practical one; and while it deals with hope, it has more to do with the result of that hope in the purity of the believer's life.

The Believer's Hope

The text speaks of men who have their "hope in him," which I understand to mean hope in Jesus Christ. *The Christian has a hope peculiar to himself.* As for its object, it is the hope of being like Jesus Christ. "We shall be like him; for we shall see him as he is." Some would not put it in that shape. They would say that their hope as Christians is to pass within the pearly gates and tread the golden streets, being forever free from sorrow, toil, and pain. But those are only the lower joys of heaven, except so far as they indicate spiritual bliss.

The real truth that is contained in these metaphors and figures and underlies them all is that the heaven a true Christian seeks after is a spiritual one—it is the heaven of being like Jesus Christ. I take it that while it will consist in our sharing in the Redeemer's power, the Redeemer's joy, and the Redeemer's honor, yet from the connection of the text, it lies mainly in our being spiritually and morally like our Redeemer—being purified, even as He is pure. I must frankly confess that of all my expectations of heaven, I will cheerfully renounce ten thousand things if I can but know that I shall have perfect holiness. If I may become like Jesus Christ as to His character—pure and perfect—I cannot understand how any other joy can be denied me. If we shall have that, surely we shall have everything. This, then, is our hope, that "we shall be like him."

Every man sees morally what he is himself. A man who is bad sees evil and is blind to good. The man who is partially like Christ has only a partial view of Christ. If your eye does not see inexpressible beauty in Him, it is your eye that is to blame, for He is altogether lovely. And when the eye of our inward nature shall come to see Jesus as He is, then we may depend upon it that we are like Him. It is the pure in heart who see God (Matt. 5:8) because God, the inexpressibly pure One, can be seen only by those who are themselves pure. When we shall be perfectly pure, we shall be able to understand Christ; and when we understand Christ, or see Him as He is, as we shall do at His appearing, then we shall be like Him—free from sin, full of consecration to God, pure and perfect. Today, He is Conqueror over sin and death and hell; He is superlative in His virtue and His holiness; He has conquered all the powers of evil; and one day we too shall put our foot on the old dragon's head, we too shall see sin crushed beneath us, and we shall come off "more than conquerors through him that loved us" (Rom. 8:37). This, then, is our hope, that we shall be like our Head when we shall see Him as He is.

But why do we expect this? *What is the ground of our hope?* The context shows us that we do not expect to be like Christ because of anything that is in us by nature or because of any efforts that we ourselves can make. The basis of all is divine love; for observe, the chapter begins: "Behold, what manner of love the Father hath bestowed upon us, that we should be called the sons of God." We expect to be like Christ, the Beloved of God, because we also are beloved of God. It is according to the nature and purpose of the love of God to make its object like God. We therefore expect that divine love will work with divine light and divine purity and make us into light and purity too.

The Apostle John goes on to say that we have been called the sons of God and that we really are God's sons. That is another ground of our hope: we hope to be like Christ because the sons of God are like each other. It is the Lord's purpose that Jesus Christ shall be the firstborn among many brethren. "For whom he did foreknow, he also did predestinate to be conformed to the image of his Son, that he might be the firstborn among many brethren" (Rom. 8:29). Since we are adopted into the divine family and are to be made like our Elder Brother, we believe that we shall be one day like the Lord Jesus Christ in the perfection of His excellence.

Then we have this further buttress for our hope—if it is not a main pillar of it—that we are now one with Jesus Christ and "when he shall appear, we shall be like him." There is an intimate connection between our souls and Christ. He was hidden from the world, and the world knew Him not; and therefore we are hidden, and the world does not know us. There is to be a day of His manifestation to angels and to men; and when He is manifested, we shall be manifested, too. Knowing that we are united to Christ by sacred mysterious bonds, we expect that when we shall see Him as He is, we shall be like Him.

Still, for simplicity's sake, it is good to say that the basis of our hope lies altogether in Him. "Every man that hath this hope *in him* purifieth himself." All true hope is the hope in Christ. If your hope lies in yourself, it is a delusion. If your hope rests upon an earthly priest and not upon this one great Apostle and High Priest of our profession, your hope is a lie. If your hope stands with one foot upon the work of Christ and the other foot upon your own resolutions or merits, your hope will fail. "Hope in him" is the only hope that can be acceptable to God, the only hope that will stand the test of your dying hour and of the day of judgment. Our hope, then, of being like Christ is a hope in Christ. We are trusting Him. If He does not make us like Himself, our hope is gone. If we ever get to heaven, it will be through Him, and through Him alone. He is our Alpha and Omega, the beginning and the end. There our hope begins, and there our hope ends. You, O Christ, are all our confidence! We know of none beside You. This, then is the believer's hope: a hope to be made like Christ, a hope based upon Christ.

The Effect That Hope Has Upon the Soul

"Every man that hath this hope in him purifieth himself." *It does not puff him up; it purifies him.* When the Lord shows a man His great love, He humbles him, lays him low; and so the expectation of heaven and of absolute perfection never exalts a man. If any man can say, "I am secure of heaven, and I am proud of it," he may take my word for it that he is secure of hell! If your religion puffs you up, puff your religion away, for it is not worth a puff. He who grows great in self-esteem through the love of God knows not the love of God in truth. O Lord, the more the glories of your love shall strike my eyes, the humbler I shall lie!

A man who has this hope of perfection in himself also finds that *it does not give him license to sin.* I have heard a thoughtless person say, "If I had a secure hope of heaven, I would live as I pleased." Perhaps *you* would; but then, *you* have not that hope, and God will not give it to you while you are in such a state that you would like to live in sin. If a Christian could live as he liked, how would he live? Why, he would live absolutely without sin. If the Lord would indulge the newborn nature of His own children with unrestricted liberty, in that liberty they would run after holiness. The unrenewed heart would like to sin, but the renewed heart quite as eagerly loves to obey the Lord. When the Lord has changed you, He can give you not only a hope but also a full assurance that that hope shall come true, and yet you will walk all the more carefully with your God, for "every man that hath this hope in him purifieth himself, even as he is pure."

This hope, then, does not puff up or lead to license. You can see why it is so. *Gratitude leads to holiness.* Any person who feels, "God has saved me, and I am on the way to being made like Christ," will also say, "Now that I owe all this to God, how can I show my gratitude to Him?" He must be a brute, he must be a devil, he must be seven thousand devils in one who would say, "God is doing all this for me, and, therefore, I will continue in sin." Well did the apostle say of such men that their damnation is just. But where there is the good hope of heaven, the man naturally says, "O my Lord, You have loved me so much and provided such a glorious portion for me hereafter? I will obey You in everything. I will serve You with my whole heart and soul. Help me to run in the way of Your commandments."

Such a man, when led of the Spirit, also feels that *holiness is in agreement with his expectations.* He expects to be like Christ. Very well, then, he says, "I will try to be like Christ. If I am to be the possessor of a perfect nature, the most natural thing is that I should begin to seek after it now." If the Lord intends to make you heirs of immortality to dwell at His right hand, does it seem right that you should now live as others do? Suppose you know that before long you will be at God's right hand. Does it not seem shameful that you should get drunk or be dishonest? King Lemuel's mother said to him, "It is not for kings, O Lemuel, it is not for kings to drink wine; nor for princes strong drink" (Prov. 31:4). And surely it is not for children of God to drink the wines of sin and go after the sweets of iniquity. It is not for royal princes, descended from the King of kings, to play with the filthy lewdnesses of this time and with the sins of earth. Surely an angel would not stoop to become a carrion crow. Neither can we suppose it congruous that he who is a brother to the Lord Jesus Christ and who is to dwell forever where Jesus is, should be found in the haunts of sin. The very natural fitness of things, under the blessing of God's Spirit, leads the child of God to purify himself, since he expects to be like Christ before long.

While we do not believe that any man actually purifies himself, yet the text states that "every man that hath this hope in him purifieth himself." We believe that the Holy Ghost purifies sinners by applying to them the precious blood of Jesus. We look to God for all purity, believing that He is the Creator of it. Still, the text also states that God the Holy Spirit so works in every man who has a true hope, that he labors to become purified and uses all possible means to overcome sin and to walk in righteousness. When a man has a true hope in Christ, he begins to purify himself by the power of the Holy Spirit.

First, *he puts away all the grosser sins.* Perhaps, before conversion, he had been unchaste, lewd in language and in acts, dishonest, or a blasphemer. Conversion does away with all that. I have sometimes been astonished and delighted when I have seen how readily these sins are put to death. They are taken out to the block and executed. I know men who had never lived a day without swearing yet never had a temptation to swear from the moment of conversion. So thoroughly does God renew the heart that these grosser sins go at once.

But there are sins of the flesh, which, though we are purged from them, will endeavor to return. Consequently, the man who has a hope of heaven will purify himself every day from them. He will hate the very thought of those sins and any expressions or actions that might tend toward them. He abhors them, he flees from them, for he knows that if he begins to dally with them, he will soon go from bad to worse. He understands that in this warfare, to fly is the truest courage; and, therefore, from such sins of the flesh he daily flees, like Joseph fled from Potiphar's wife, that he may get away from them. So he "purifieth himself."

Then *he purifies himself from all evil company.* Those people that he once thought great company he avoids. If they will go with him to heaven, he will be glad that they should join his side. But if they will neither repent of sin nor believe in Jesus, he says to them, "You can be of no service to me." If he can help them to heaven, he seeks them out and tries to win them; but when they ridicule him, he is afraid lest their example be injurious to him, and he shuns them, seeking better company. So he "purifieth himself."

Then *he begins from that day forth and until he dies to purify himself.* Perhaps he does not know some things to be sin that he afterwards finds out to be so. As the light gradually shines into his soul, he puts away this and that and the other with a strong and resolute hand. If there was some sin that pleased him much, that was valued by him like a right hand or a right eye, he cuts it off or tears it out (Matt. 5:29–30); for having a hope of heaven in him, he knows he cannot take any sin to heaven, and he does not want to do so. He puts it away. He knows that he must put it away before he can enter into life eternal.

Soon he finds out that there are certain sins in his nature that more readily overcome him than any others do. Against these he sets a double guard. Possibly, he has a quick temper. Over this he grieves very much and earnestly prays, "O Lord, subdue my evil temper! Guard my tongue, lest I say bitter words, and my heart, lest I indulge in unkind feelings." He finds himself in a certain business, and if in such a business there is sin, he feels, "Then I will have nothing to do with it. If I cannot make money without sin, I will lose money or change my business, but I will not do what is wrong." He observes some sin that runs in his family. Here again he cries to God, "Lord, purify me and purify my house from this evil thing!" He observes that there are certain sins in the area where he lives. Against these he cries aloud. He knows that there are sins peculiar to his position. Is he rich? He is afraid of growing worldly. Is he poor? He is afraid of becoming envious. He looks at his position and observes what the peculiar sins of that position are, and then in the power of the Eternal Spirit, he seeks to purify himself from these sins.

Is the Christian in a great trial? Then he knows the temptation to impatience and murmuring will come, and he tries to purify himself from that. Has he great pleasure? Then he knows the temptation will be to make this world his home, and so he tries to purify himself from that. You see, under the power of God's Spirit, this purifying of the life is a great work to be done, but it is a work that every man that has this hope in Christ will do. If he is indeed hoping in the Lord Jesus, this will be the great struggle and warfare of his life—to first get rid of this sin, and then that he may be wholly sanctified unto the Lord, a holy man, fitted for a holy heaven.

But how does he purify himself? I have shown you what he does, but by what means does he do it? *He does it, first, by noting the example of Christ.* The hoping man reads Christ's life and says, "Here is my model, but I am far short of it. O God, give me all that there is in Christ! Take off from my character all that is not like Him." Familiarizing himself with the life of his Savior and getting to commune with Christ, he is helped to see what sin is and where sin is, and to hate it.

Then *he prays that God will give him a tender conscience.* I wish that all Christians had tender consciences! It is a blessed thing to have a conscience that will shiver when the very ghost of a sin goes by, a conscience that is not like our great ships at sea that do not yield to every wave, but like a cork on the water that goes up and down with every ripple, sensitive in a moment to the very approach of sin. May God the Holy Spirit make us so! This sensitiveness the Christian endeavors to have, for he knows that if he does not have it, he will never be purified from sin.

He tries to always keep an eye to God and not to men. That is a great point in purity of life. I know many persons whose main thought concerns other people's opinions. Their question is, "What will So-and-so say? What will the neighbors say? What will be thought of it?" You will never be holy until you do not care a fig what anybody says except your God, for a thing that is right is right anywhere. If it is right before the Lord, it is right although all the world should hiss it down. Oh, that we had more moral courage, for moral courage is essential to true holiness! The man who has this hope in Him will not say, "If the door is shut and nobody hears of it, I may feel free to do evil." No. Such hypocrisy shows a rotten heart. The man of God will say, "This is right before the Lord, and though no eye sees me to commend men, and though every tongue should speak against me, I will do the right thing." This is one way in which the Christian "purifieth himself."

And then *he notes the lives of others and makes them his beacons.* If you were sailing down the Thames and saw a boat ahead of you run upon a shoal, there would be no reason for you to go there to find out where the true channel was. The other shipwrecks would be your beacons. So the Christian, when he observes a fault in another, does not stand and say, "Ah, see how faulty that man is!" Rather he says, "Let me shun that fault." And when he sees the virtue of another, if his heart is right, he does not begin to pick holes in it and say, "He is not as good as he looks." Rather he says, "Lord, there is a sweet flower in that man's garden, give me some of the seed of it; let it grow in my soul." So other men become both his beacon and his example.

A wise Christian tries to purify himself *by listening to a heart-searching ministry.* If the ministry never cuts you, it is of no use to you. If it does not make you feel ashamed of yourself and sometimes half angry with the preacher, it is not good for much. If it is all smoothing you the way the feathers go, making you feel happy and comfortable, be afraid of it. But if, on the contrary, it seems to open up old wounds and make the sores fester and the soul bleed before the living God, then you may hope it is a ministry that God is using for your lasting good. Not only does the true Christian wish the preacher to search him, but his prayer is, "Search me, O God, and know my heart: try me, and know my thoughts" (Ps. 139:23). He does not want to live in sin, thinking it not to be sin, but he wants to get away from it. I am afraid some Christians do not want to know too many of Christ's commands; there might be some awkward ones, and they do not want to attend to some of them. They are very pleased if they can get some minister to say that some of Christ's commands are nonessential and unimportant. Ah, he is a traitor to his Master if he dares to say anything like that. It is always important for a servant to do as his Master tells him, and it is essential to comfort and to obedience that whatever the Lord has spoken we endeavor to perform in His strength.

I might continue to show you the way by which the Christian endeavors to purify himself, but I must notice this one thing, that *he sets before himself the standard of Christ.* He purifies himself, even as Christ is pure. We shall make a mistake if we make anyone our model save the Lord Jesus, for in any other life but His there will be sure to be something in excess. I am sure it will be best for us, if we are Wesleyans, not always to try to do everything as John Wesley did it; and if we are Calvinists, much as we honor John Calvin, to remember that we shall go wrong if we try to season everything with the spirit of John Calvin. No man is fit to be a model for all men except the Savior who redeemed men.

In white, all the colors are blended. A perfectly white substance combines all the colors of the rainbow merged in true proportion, but green and indigo and red are only the reflections of a part of the solar rays. So John, Peter, and Paul are parts of the light of heaven; they are differing colors, and there is a beauty in each of them. But if you want to get the whole of the rays of light, you must get to Christ, for all light is in Him. In Him is not simply the red or the blue, but in Him is light, the true light, the whole of light. You are sure to get a lopsided character if any man shall be the copy after which you write. If we copy Christ, we shall, through the power of His Spirit, attain to perfect manhood.

What a life-task is here for you! "Every man that hath this hope in him purifieth himself, even as he is pure." We shall never be able to throw down our weapons and say, "Now I have no more sin to fight with, no more evil to overcome." I have heard of some brethren who say that, but I think it must be a mistake. If there is a possibility of getting to that condition, I mean to get to it, and I would recommend you try as well; but I think that until you die, you will have some evil to struggle with. As long as you are in this body, there will be enough tinder for one of the devil's sparks to set it afire. You will have need to keep on damping it and every moment be on the watchtower, even till you cross the Jordan. This is our life's business, and I do not know that you can have a better business, for while you are contending against sin, purifying yourself by the precious blood of Jesus, you will be bringing honor and glory to God. Your heart will become a field in which the power and grace of God will be displayed, for He will come and purify you; He will be the real Purifier while He is using you to purify yourself.

Use the Text as a Test

"Every man that hath this hope in him purifieth himself." The question is, Do we have a true hope in Christ? If we have, we purify ourselves—we labor to purify ourselves even as Christ is pure.

Some professors of faith do the opposite to this—*they defile themselves*. It is a shame that I should have to say it. They were baptized on profession of their faith, but they were never cleansed from their sins. I have heard of people who come to the communion table yet go to the table of the drunkard, too. How can anyone say they have a true hope in Christ if they love such sin? We must not deceive ourselves and lie. If you are not pure and chaste, you are none of God's children. You may fall into sin by surprise, but if you calmly and deliberately go to that which is unclean, how does the love of God dwell in you?

"He that committeth sin is of the devil" (1 John 3:8). It is no use making excuses and apologies. If you are a lover of sin, you shall go where sinners go. If you who live after this fashion say that you have believed in the precious blood of Jesus, I do not believe you. If you had a true faith in that precious blood, you would hate sin. If you dare to say you are trusting in the atonement while you live in sin, you lie. After all, holiness is *the* test. So let the great fan throw up the chaff and the wheat together, and let the wind go through it and blow the chaff away. Some come to church and sit as God's people but are a disgrace to the profession they make. May God forgive them and give them grace to repent of their sin and come to Christ! This is, after all, the test: "Every man that hath this hope in him purifieth himself." How can he have that hope in Him if he defiles himself?

There are others who, while they do not actually defile themselves, *let things go very much as a matter of course*. They do not purify themselves, certainly, but they go with the flow of the stream. If there is a good tone at home, they do not object to it; if there is an evil one, they do not rebuke it. If they are in the shop and someone speaks upon religion, they chime in. If anybody ridiculed it, perhaps they would not join in, but they say nothing. They never take sides with Christ, except when everybody else is on His side. True, they do not take sides with the devil, but they mean to be neutral.

Such a person will slip, one of these days, into his appointed place in hell. He knows better, he proves his knowledge by a little sneaking affection to the right, and yet he cleaves to the evil. The dead fish that floats down the stream has only one fault, but down the stream it goes for that one fault. The man who gives himself up to the current in which he is, proves himself to be spiritually dead. Did you never put your foot down and say, "I will not do this"? Others have to fight to win the crown, and you expect to get it by lying in bed. Do you think there are crowns in heaven for those who never fight their sins? Do you believe that there are rewards in heaven for those who never followed Christ and endured hardship for His sake?

The truth is in that famous picture of John Bunyan's. He tells us that the Pilgrim saw, in the Interpreter's house, a beautiful palace. On the top of it there walked many people clothed in gold, and from the roof there came the sweetest music that mortal ear had ever heard. He felt that he would give anything to be on the top of that palace with those who so happily basked in the sun. So he went to see the way but found at the door that there stood a number of armed men who pushed back every person who sought to enter. Then he stood back in amazement. But he noted that there sat one at a table having a writer's ink-horn, and a brave man from the crowd, of stout countenance, came up and said, "Set down my name, sir!" And when his name was set down on the roll, he at once drew his sword and began to cut his way through the armed men. The fight was long and cruel, and he was wounded; but he did not give up the conflict till he had cut his way through, making a living lane through those who opposed him. So he pressed his way in, and the singers on the top of the palace welcomed him with sweet music, singing, "Come in, come in! Eternal glory thou shalt win."

If you would go to heaven, it is all of grace through the precious blood of Christ. It is all by simple faith in Christ, yet every person who gets there must fight for it. There is no crown except for warriors; there are no rewards except for those who contend for the mastery against flesh and blood, against Satan, and against sin. Are you one of stout countenance whom God has made resolute against sin? Then set your name down. Only remember that he who puts on his harness must not boast as though he were putting it off. There is much that you will never perform except the Eternal God be at your back. Nevertheless, if you have this hope in you, if you have received this hope from God, if it is a hope based upon divine sonship, upon divine love, a "hope in *him*," you shall win the day. You shall purify yourself, even as He is pure; and when He shall appear, you shall be like Him, for you shall see Him as He is.

Have you ever looked at a green field and thought how bright the sparkling dewdrops are? Did you ever then turn your eye on the sun and look at it and try to stare it out of brightness? If you have, I know what has happened, for when you looked down upon the landscape again, you could not see it. You seemed to have lost your eyesight, the eye having been put out by the brightness on which it gazed. So you may look on the world of sin and see some beauty in it till you look at HIM, and then the brightness of His glory puts out your eye. The world is dark and black after that, and you wish it so to be. Let these eyes be forever sightless as the eyes of night, and let these ears be forever deaf as silence, rather than sin should have a charm for me or anything should take up my spirit save the Lord of love, who bled Himself to death that He might redeem me.

Chapter Six

Death for Sin, and Death to Sin

Who his own self bare our sins in his own body on the tree, that we, being dead to sins, should live unto righteousness: by whose stripes ye were healed—1 Peter 2:24.

PETER IN THIS CHAPTER exhorted Christians to holiness and emphasized that branch of holiness that consists in the patient endurance of wrong. He could find no better argument with which to plead with the saints than the life and example of their Lord, and indeed, who could? Since the Lord Jesus is all our salvation, He is also all our desire, and to be like Him is the highest object of our lives. If, therefore, we find Him patient under wrong, it is to us a conclusive argument that we should be patient also.

I admire the Apostle Peter, because in using such an excellent argument he selected from the life of his Lord that particular portion of it that must have been most vividly written upon his own soul. Consider whether I am correct in this. Which hour of the sufferings of the Lord—from Gethsemane to Golgotha—would be most deeply engraven upon the memory of Peter? Surely it would be that space of time in which Jesus was mocked and buffeted in the hall of the high priest. While Peter sat warming his hands at the fire, he saw his Lord abused and was afraid to declare that he was His disciple, becoming so terrified that with profane language he declared, "I know not the man." So long as life lingered, the Apostle Peter would remember the meek and quiet bearing of his suffering Lord. He alluded to it in the twenty-third verse: "When he was reviled, reviled not again; when he suffered, he threatened not; but committed himself to him that judgeth righteously." Many a tear had Peter to brush out of his eye as he wrote that verse. He recollected having seen the Lord with his own eyes, and so he mentioned as an argument with others that which was the most forcible upon his own mind, hoping that whenever they were misjudged or falsely accused, they might remember their Lord and like Him be dumb as a sheep before her shearers and silent as a lamb led to the slaughter.

Lest, however, we should think that the patience of the Lord was intended to be our example and nothing more, the apostle goes on to speak expressly of the expiatory nature of the sufferings alluded to. He has held up the Savior in all His woes as our example, but knowing the evil tendency of skeptical minds by any means to take away the value of the cross, he now puts aside the example for a moment and speaks of the Redeemer as the great sacrifice for sin. The sacred writers are always very clear and distinct upon this truth, and so must we be. There is no preaching the gospel if the atonement is left out. No matter how well we speak of Jesus as an example, we have done nothing unless we point Him out as the substitute and sin bearer. We must, in fact, continually imitate the apostle and speak plainly of Him "who his own self bare our sins in his own body on the tree."

It is to Christ as the sin bearer that I direct your attention. I have felt that if any theme in the Scriptures has an importance far above all the rest, it is the subject of the atoning blood, and I have resolved to repeat that old, old story again and again. Though I may be guilty of tautologies, I shall keep on sounding this silver trumpet and ringing this golden bell. So when I am dead and gone the way of all flesh, you will perhaps say, his fault was that he dwelt too much on his favorite subject, the substitution of Christ. Ah, may I have no other fault to account for, for that shall be accounted to be one of my highest virtues! I would know nothing among men save Jesus Christ and Him crucified. At the same time, we shall try to make our subject practical, because the second half of our text suggests the way by which the great sacrifice for sin leads us to make a slaughter of sin, telling us that when Christ puts sin away *for* us, we are moved to put away sin *from* us.

Our Lord's Death for Sin

May the Holy Spirit help us to behold that wondrous sight of the Redeemer dying in our place, a sacrifice for our sin. But before we approach to behold the great sight, let us put off our shoes from our feet and bow down in lowliest reverence of repenting grief, for remember, if Jesus had not died for sins, we must have died—and died eternally. The pains of the Savior on the cross surpassed all estimate, but such as they were, they must have tormented us, if they had not put Him to anguish. That cup that made Him sweat in the garden was bitter beyond imagination, but to your lips and to mine it must have been set: unable as we should have been to drain it dry, we must have continued to drink thereof forever and forever. "In the day that thou eatest thereof thou shalt surely die" is the great sentence against sin (Gen. 2:17), and for a soul to die is a terrible doom. Our great father, Adam, felt the first drops of the dreadful shower of death in the moment that he ate of the forbidden fruit, for he died to God and holiness and virtue and true happiness in that same hour, standing aghast before his God, before that very God whom at other times he had met with rapture and adored with delight.

As Adam's children, in our depraved natures we share in his spiritual death, and we should soon have passed away from the present death of this time-state to that corruption that naturally follows upon death in the world to come. Yes, were it not for Him "who his own self bare our sins in his own body on the tree," I would have been compelled to tell you that there remained nothing for any one of us but to die and to endure the wrath of God in body and soul, world without end. Oh, the bitterness of our souls had we been in such a state! With anguish of spirit, I might have been compelled to utter more woes than ever fell from the lips of Jeremiah, from whom all joy was gone, while I declared to you and your children that there was no hope here or hereafter, that we had offended God, and that He had given us over to utter destruction.

Blessed be His name, we have another message to deliver now! We may rather imitate Isaiah today than Jeremiah and tell of redeeming grace and dying love instead of having to sound the dreadful knell of every hope and to proclaim the birth of legions of sorrows. With this fact upon our mind, let us come lovingly to the blessed place of Calvary, once cursed on our account. *Jesus died for me*—fix that as your uppermost feeling.

There was a substitution for our sins, and by that substitution, believers are saved. "His own self bare our sins in his own body on the tree." A substitute intervened so that the sins that would have crushed us were borne by another, actually and literally borne by another. "His own self bare our sins." The sentence means that He bare the punishment that was due to our sins. We are sure it means that, but surely it means more. In that wonderful gospel chapter of Isaiah, we are told, "The LORD hath laid on him the iniquity of us all," and again, "He bare the sin of many" (Isa. 53:6, 12). It does seem as if the bearing of the punishment, great as that is, would not exhaust the meaning of such phrases. The expression is so compact, so concise, so definite, it must mean what it says. At any rate, I am content to believe that God knows how to speak and express His own meaning, and that the less we twist the Scriptures or get away from the simple sense that they would suggest to a child, the more likely we are to understand them. "His own self bare our sins"—in some wondrous sense He bore the sin as well as the punishment. I know not how. This I know, He never was a sinner, for "in him was no sin." This I know, He never was defiled; it could not be. He, the Son of God, the immaculate Man, stained with sin? Never! We abhor the thought. And yet "He bare our sins" is still a truth, and we must not flinch from it.

Does it not mean that He was a representative person? He was the Second Adam, and therefore He stood for His people. The Lord dealt with Him as if the sins of all He represented had been His own sins. He was the Shepherd, and the Lord called upon Him to give an account for the flock. All the wanderings of all the sheep and all their transgressions, divine justice visited upon the Shepherd's head, because He was by office and by nature the representative of all those for whom He died, and so could justly be called to account for all that they had done. Sin was laid upon the Lord Jesus, for He was forsaken of His God. The Lord did not merely chasten Him and scourge Him and put Him to grief by the use of agencies that were suitable for such a purpose in an innocent person, but He went further and hid His face from Jesus, which was a sorrow fitting only for one upon whom sin was laid. Why should God forsake Him, unless He had laid sin upon Him first? When Jesus said, "My God, my God, why hast thou forsaken me?" (Mark 15:34), there was no answer to that cry except this one (at least I cannot imagine another), "I have laid sin upon You, and therefore I must forsake You."

If He were merely suffering for others in the sense of doing others good by His sufferings, the Father might surely have looked upon Him with complacency and even, if possible, with increased delight and have encouraged Him in the benevolent disinterestedness that made Him stoop to such sufferings. But inasmuch as He was not only enduring for others but also enduring in the place of others and bearing their sins, it became needful that—despite the love of the Father and the admiration that glowed in His bosom toward His dear Son, who was then above all things magnifying the nature of God the Father—regarding Jesus as bearing sin, the Father must hide His face from Him and smite Him with the blows of a cruel one till He cried out, *"Eloi, Eloi, lama sabachthani?"* Yes, there was a substitution, and that substitution went mysteriously far. It was not merely a transfer of punishment from one to another, but there was a transfer of sin in some deep sense.

Having noted the fact of substitution, I want you to *consider the substitute.* "His own self bare our sins." I want you to feel a personal love to our dear Lord and Master. I want your soul at this moment to realize the actual character of His existence and His true personality. He is not here in person to show Himself to you, else I might very well withhold my words, for His presence would have an infinitely superior power over you. But remember that He lives and is as real as you are and at this moment bears in His body the scars of His sufferings for you. Consider, then, who He was, and let your spirits kiss His feet in humble contrite love. He who bare our sins in His own body on the tree was God over all, blessed forever, of whom and through whom and by whom are all things. Less than God could not have borne your sin so as to put it away; but the infinitely glorious Son of God did actually stoop to become a sin bearer.

It is a truth scarcely to be declared in words. It wants flame and blood and tears with which to tell this story of an offended God, the Heaven Maker and the Earth Creator, stooping from His glory that He might save the reptiles that had dared to insult His honor and rebel against glory. And, becoming one of them, to suffer for them, that without violation of His law He might have pity upon the offending things—things so inconsiderable that if He had stamped them all out, as men burn a nest of wasps, there had been no loss to the universe. But He had pity on them, becoming one of them, and bare their sins. Oh, let us love and adore Him. Let your soul climb up to the right hand of the Majesty above and there bow in lowliest reverence and adoring affection, that He, the God over all, whom you had offended, should His own self bear our sins. Though thus God over all, He became a man like unto ourselves. A body was prepared for Him, and that body was not otherwise fashioned than ourselves. He came into the world as we also come—born of a woman, a child of a real mother—not merely like to man, but man, born in the pedigree of manhood, and so bone of our bone and flesh of our flesh, yet without a taint of sin. And He, in that double nature but united person, was Jesus, Son of God and Son of the Virgin.

Here we call to your remembrance the fact stated in the text so positively, that *the substitution of Christ was carried out by Him personally*, not by proxy. "His own self bare our sins in his own body." The Old Testament priest brought a substitution, but it was a lamb. He struck the knife, and the warm blood flowed from it, but our Lord Jesus Christ had no substitute for Himself. O thou Priest of God! The pangs are to be Your own pangs; the knife must reach Your own heart. No lamb for You; You are the Lamb. The blood that streams at Your feet must be Your own blood: wounds there must be, but they must be wounds in Your own flesh.

Turn your loving eyes to your Lord and behold that everything He did for you He did Himself. Consider His personal sacrifice for you: the griefs that Jesus bore put His own soul into a tempest of grief and made His own heart to boil like a cauldron with Him. The heart that was broken for our sin was His own heart, and the life given up was His own life. Not by another, though he were an angel, could Christ have redeemed mankind.

Notice also that *the substitution of Christ is described in a way that suggests consciousness, willinghood, and great pain.* "His own self bare our sins." They were upon Him, they pressed Him. The Greek word for *bare* suggests the idea of a great weight. "He bare our sins"—stooped under them, as it were; our sins were a load to Him. Our Lord assumed our sins as one takes a weight upon his shoulders; and when the sins were there, He knew that He was carrying our burdens and consented to do so. There was not a moment in Christ's life in which the pressure of sin was unfelt. Though the wrath of God on account of sin was more especially felt by Him at Gethsemane and Calvary, yet at all times He was stricken, smitten of God, and afflicted. What a weight was this! The solid earth cannot bear the weight of sin; it groans and travails in pain together until now, like a creaking chariot whose axles are unable to bear up under the stupendous freight. Yet on Jesus was the burden laid, a far weightier one than the fabled Atlas bore, and He sustained it to the tree.

The text, in our English version, might seem to teach that our Lord bore our sins only on the tree, and that erroneous dogma has been drawn from it. No inference could have been more feebly sustained, for the original language does not necessarily set forth anything of the kind. The word translated "on" is precisely the same word that in the next verse is translated "to" or "unto"—"are now returned *unto*"—and might have been just as correctly read "unto" in this case. I have not the slightest doubt that the meaning of the text is, "His own self bare our sins in his own body to the tree," so that when He reached the tree, He left our sins there, condemned and crucified forever and ever. Instead of the doctrine being deduced that Christ only on the tree was a substitute, the fact is He always was a substitute up to the tree, and there and then that substitution culminated in His dying as a sin offering. From the time He was a babe in Bethlehem till the moment when He bowed His head and gave up the ghost, "His own self bare our sins in his own body to the tree."

And, *He bore those sins manifestly.* I think that is the mind of the Spirit when He says "in his own body," He means to give vividness to the thought. We are so constituted that we do not think so forcibly of mental and spiritual things as we do of bodily things; but our Lord bare our sins "in his own body." If you had looked at Him, had you been instructed by the Spirit, you would have seen in His body that He was a sin bearer. Listen to this verse: "As many were astonied at thee; his visage was so marred more than any man, and his form more than the sons of men" (Isa. 52:14). Remember another text: "Yet we did esteem him stricken, smitten of God" (Isa. 53:4). Think of that! Those who looked into the Savior's face thought Him "smitten of God." First they thought Him stricken or demented, like one who has passed through such an awful sorrow that the mind has quailed beneath it, and then they looked at Him as smitten of God. Even the Jews judged Him to be near to fifty when He was hardly thirty years of age, so worn and haggard did He look, that "man of sorrows, and acquainted with grief" (Isa. 53:3). He smiled and He cheered others, wearing a cheerful countenance among the sons of men that He might not make those sorrowful around Him. Deep down in His heart there glowed a secret fire, a wondrous joy that He was redeeming His own chosen; but still imponderable, incomprehensible infinite griefs perpetually rolled over Him, so that all His lifetime He might have said, "All thy waves and thy billows are gone over me" (Ps. 42:7).

And when He came to the cross, oh, how His body bore our sin, then in communion with His sinless soul! I do not care who it is that speaks against descriptions of the crucifixion or who would have us keep in the background the bodily sufferings of Jesus, I am persuaded that the highest, most intense, and most forceful godliness that ever existed among men has arisen out of contemplations of the agony of Gethsemane and the death throes of Calvary. Despite all its errors, the Catholic Church has always had in her midst a band of loving, adoring spirits who have entered into the Redeemer's passion and whose meat and drink have been the flesh and blood of Christ in their silent contemplations. If Protestant Christians ever fall into the idea that we must not think too much of the blood and wounds of Jesus, they will lose the richest spiritual sustenance, and we shall cease to have eminent saints among us. I shall not be ashamed at any time to talk to you of the bodily griefs of Jesus, when I remember that Peter, or rather the Holy Ghost by Peter, puts it so in the text: "Who his own self bare our sin in *his own body* to the tree."

There is the cross, and there is the body. There are the visible things as well as the spiritual and the unseen. We will not forget the second, but we will by no means ever despise the first, but will speak lovingly and tenderly of the body and of the bodily sufferings of the Lord. Look then to the Lord of life and glory taken outside the city gate of old Jerusalem and there amidst a ribald throng treated as a common criminal. It was where felons were usually executed; and they took our Master and treated Him as a felon. They nail His hands! See the cruel iron is driven through His feet! They lift Him up, a spectacle of shame. They have stripped Him. They have gambled over the few garments that He had, and there He hangs. They gather round Him, and they mock Him, as if the cross were a place of contempt as well as a place of execution. They insult Him with studied sarcasm, and He has no reply to make except to bless them with His prayers and to appeal to His God. His friends have fled, and when they timidly return, they can only share His sorrow, but they cannot alleviate it. He must die, die in extreme pain of body, and die with unknown inward agonies, the veil of which we will not attempt to lift. "His own self bare our sins in His own body on the tree." Blessed are You, O Savior, and blessed are the eyes that have seen You and have looked to You by faith.

Now our Lord Jesus Christ, be it remembered, never ceased to bear our sins till He had taken them right up to the tree, and when He had taken them to the tree, there He hung them on the cross forever as a spectacle of eternal scorn. He died while He made our sins to die; Himself crucified while He crucified our sins once for all. It was a shameful thing to die the death of the cross, and yet our Lord bore it completely.

Mark the tree of a cross for a moment with much attention. It was the place of *pain*. No death could be more full of agony than that of crucifixion. When the headsman's axe falls on the neck, the head is severed and the pain is over, but the pain of the crucifixion may last days. Cases have been known in which men have actually lived after a three days' nailing to a cross. The pain itself is inconceivably great. The tenderest parts of the hands and feet, where they are most likely to bring on lockjaw, being torn by the nails, and the strain of the body continued tearing at the wounds. Yet our Savior bore that pain. It is not till you suffer pain that you begin to know the love of Christ to the full. You may thank Him, you sons of sorrow and daughters of suffering, for all your pangs, for now you have fellowship with Him. Blessed be Your love, O Jesus, that You could bear pain and death for us.

But the cross was not the place of pain merely, it was the place of *scorn*. To be fastened to the cross! They would not put the meanest Roman on a cross, though he committed murder. Crucifixion was a death for slaves and menials. When scorn mingles with pain, you know what a compound of grief it makes. To be laughed at when you suffer is to suffer sevenfold.

But more, it was the place of *the curse*, for "cursed is every one that hangeth on a tree," and the Word has told us that he was "made a curse for us" (Gal. 3:13).

Last of all, it was the place of *death*, for Jesus must not merely bleed, but bleed to death; nor suffer only, but suffer till life itself was gone. O dying Savior, Your love to me was wonderful, for death itself could not turn it aside, and therefore blessed, forever blessed, be Your name.

Before we leave the cross, let the believer sit down and see on the cross his sins hanging up as dead. Christ carried them up to the cross and slew them. The law comes to me and says, "I arrest you for sin," but I reply, "I have no sin. What would you do with my sins if I had any?" "I would put them to a shameful death." "Lo, they are yonder, executed upon the accursed tree by Jesus Christ." Look, then, at your sins hanged upon the cross, abhor and loathe them, but rejoice that loathsome as they are, they are dead. The Lord put them all to death and put sin away forever by His death upon the tree. The death of Jesus is the death of our sins.

You cannot make recompense to God for your sin, either by repentance or by future reformation. Your only hope is to look to Jesus Christ, who bore the sins of His people in His own body on the tree; and if you will come and put your trust in Jesus, your sin shall be put away from you, and you shall be accepted.

Our Death to Sin

"Who his own self bare our sins in his own body on the tree, that we, being dead to sins, should live unto righteousness: by whose stripes ye were healed." Correctly observe that we are dead to the condemning power of sin. No sin can condemn a believer in Jesus Christ, because Christ has suffered what we should have suffered on account of sin. He has rendered a full recompense to divine justice. You bring me a large file full of bills, and you say to me, "Are not these bills against you?" I answer, "No doubt they are all correct in every item." You ask me, "Can you pay them?" "No, and I do not need to try." "But do they not trouble you?" "No. I can make a pillow of them if that is all, and sleep notwithstanding their number and greatness." You are wonder struck to think that I should have such a mass of bills and take the matter so coolly. I ask you to take off these bills from the file one by one, and as you do so, you see that they are all receipted: there is a red mark at the bottom of every one. Who troubles himself about a bill when it is paid? "But did you pay those debts?" "No. I have not paid a penny." "Did you not pay part of them?" "Not I. I never contributed a dime toward them." "Yet you are perfectly at rest?" "Yes, because He who bore my sins in His own body on the tree, took all my debts and paid them for me, and now I am dead to these debts; they have no power over me. I have nothing to do with them. They are gone as much as if they had never been committed. Henceforth I have nothing to do but to live as a righteous man, accepted in the Beloved, to live by His righteousness and rejoice in it, blessing and magnifying His Holy name."

Please hear the text again. Anyone who has looked to Jesus Christ bearing his sins in His own body on the tree is dead to sin as to its reigning power. Dead because we have seen its detestable nature. The sin that was so evil that it required the Son of God Himself to die before it could be pardoned is too awful and desperate an evil for us to dally with it anymore. It had its charms, but now we have perceived its hypocrisies. The false prophet Mokanna, who wore the silver veil upon his brow, deceived many, for he said that should that veil be lifted, the light that would gleam from under it would strike men blind, the glory was so great. But when one had once perceived that the man was leprous and that on his brow instead of brightness there were the white scales of a leper, nobody would become his disciple. And so, O sin, at the cross I see thy silver veil removed, and I mark the desperate leprosy that is on you. I am dead to you. Begone, you foul, bloodstained traitor! I cannot harbor you in my heart. The death of Christ, then, is to us the death of sin.

We are dead to sin, because another passion has absorbed all the forces of our life. Have you never seen men dead to other things because another passion has eaten them up? Look at the miser: ask him why he does not eat a full meal. He is dead to his appetite. Tempt him with rich wines; bring before him the dainties of the season. They will cost him money, and he wants them not. He tells you he has no taste or love for such things. But you tell him that there is sweet music to be heard and there are pleasures to be enjoyed. Yes, but there must be money paid out for them, and therefore he has no ear and no eye. His own dear gold is everything. He is dead to everything else. But there is rent due from a poor widow with many children, and he will seize her goods and turn her out upon the cold stones of the street. Tell him of the widow and her tears, of the orphans and their woes. What does he care? He asks you whether you ever had any house property and assures you that if you had you would soon have as hard a heart as he has. But has the man no compassion? No, sir. He has no life except that which pulsates to the chink of his money bags. The zeal of his gold has eaten him up. It is just so with us as to Christ. We have no eyes or ears for anything but for our dear Lord, who bled and died and is gone up into His glory. Now sin may charm, but we have the adder's ear; sin may put on all its allurements, but we are blind as bats to its beauty, and we wish to be. We are dead to sin; so says the text. Another passion has sucked up our life, and our life for sin is all dried up.

And yet sin appears to us now to be too mean and trivial a thing for us to care about. Picture Paul going along the Appian Way toward Rome, met by some of the Christians far away at Puteoli, and afterward by others at the Three Taverns. Can you imagine what they talked about as Paul walked along the highway? They would commune concerning Jesus, and the resurrection, and the Spirit, and saints converted, and souls in heaven. I can conceive that the soldiers and others who would come up with them would have many things to talk about. One of them would say, "There will be a grand fight at the amphitheater next week." And another would say, "Oh, but over at such a theater there is a splendid show—a hundred beasts are to be slain in a single night, and the famous German gladiator is to exhibit his prowess tomorrow evening." Others would babble about a thousand things. But the apostle would be supremely indifferent to it all. Not a topic that any one of those soldiers could bring before him or any of the people around him could interest him. He was dead to the things to which they were alive and alive to the things to which they were dead. So is the Christian. The cross has killed him, and the cross has given him life. We are dead to sin that we should live unto righteousness. Now our very power to enjoy sin, if indeed we are resting in Christ, is gone from us. We have lost now, by God's grace, the faculty that once was gratified with these things. The world tells us we deny ourselves many pleasures. Oh, there is a sense in which a Christian lives a self-denying life, but there is another sense in which he practices no self-denial at all, for he only denies himself what he does not want, what he would not have if he could. If you could force it upon him, it would be misery to him—his views and tastes are now so changed.

Have you ever looked at a green field and thought how bright the sparkling dewdrops are? Did you ever then turn your eye on the sun and look at it and try to stare it out of brightness? If you have, I know what has happened, for when you looked down upon the landscape again, you could not see it. You seemed to have lost your eyesight, the eye having been put out by the brightness on which it gazed. So you may look on the world of sin and see some beauty in it till you look at HIM, and then the brightness of His glory puts out your eye. The world is dark and black after that, and you wish it so to be. Let these eyes be forever sightless as the eyes of night, and let these ears be forever deaf as silence, rather than sin should have a charm for me or anything should take up my spirit save the Lord of love, who bled Himself to death that He might redeem me.

This is the royal road to sanctification. The death of Christ becomes the death of sin. We see Him bleed for us, and then we put our sin to death. And it seems to me, as if the last sentence of our text told us this—"by whose stripes ye were healed." It is as good as if the Spirit said, "There is the recipe for sanctification. If you want to know how to be dead to sin and alive unto righteousness, there it is. His stripes will heal you." The wales, the blue marks of His scourgings, these will take out the lines of sin. The wounds, the sweat, the death throes of the Savior, these will cure you of sin's disease. We think that the cure for sin is to give something out from ourselves and to do some good thing; but in truth the cure for sin is "Take." Take what? Take your dear Lord's wounds and trust them; take His griefs and rest in them; take His death and believe in it; take Himself and love Him, and by His stripes you are healed. Sanctification is by faith in Jesus Christ. We overcome through the blood of the Lamb. And as the topmost stone is stained with the blood, so must the foundation stone be.

I pray that the Spirit of God may show you what it is to believe alone in Him "who his own self bare our sins in his own body on the tree." If you do, though your sins have been as scarlet, they shall be as wool; though you have been the most atrocious offender existing on the face of the earth, you shall be absolutely clean from every sin. You may have been as black as hell but shall be as pure as the white-robed hosts in heaven if you can but believe in Jesus. This is the washing in the fountain, the fountain that alone can make us clean. God help us to wash immediately, lest the time for washing be past and the time for judgment be come.

Observe that this law of the house is not only intense, reaching to the superlative degree of holiness, but it is most sweeping and encompassing, for we read, "Upon the top of the mountain the whole limit thereof round about shall be most holy." The outer courts, the courts of the Gentiles, the walls, the promenades outside the walls, the slopes of the hill, every part that had to do with the mountain upon which the temple stood, was to be most holy. From which I gather that in the church of God it is not merely her ministers that are to be most holy, but all her members—not her sacraments only, but her ordinary meals; not her Sabbaths only, but her workdays; not her worship only, but her daily labor. All that surrounds our consecrated life is to be consecrated, too. The secular matters that touch our religion are to be made religious—whether we eat or drink or "whatsoever ye do in word or deed, do all in the name of the Lord Jesus" (Col. 3:17). Not only are the bells on the high priest's garments to be "holiness unto the Lord," but the bells of the horses are to be the same. The pots and bowls of our kitchens are to be as truly sacred as the golden vessels with which the priest served the altar of the Most High. Holiness should cover the whole ground of a Christian's life. The Christian should be sanctified "spirit, soul, and body," and in all things he should bear evidence of having been set apart to the Lord. Paul prayed that "the very God of peace sanctify you wholly" (1 Thess. 5:23). Amen; so let it be.

Chapter Seven

Holiness, the Law of God's House

This is the law of the house; Upon the top of the mountain the whole limit thereof round about shall be most holy. Behold, this is the law of the house—Ezekiel 43:12.

I SHALL NOT ENTER into the immediate meaning of Ezekiel's vision. I believe that the house of which Ezekiel speaks is typical of the church of the living God. In it I see not so much the visible church as that spiritual, mystical church of Jesus Christ that is the one place of His abode. It is found in a state of grace on earth and in full glory in heaven. Below it is the holy church militant; above it is the holy church triumphant.

The church is the only thing upon earth that can properly be called the house of God, for He does not dwell in temples made with hands, that is to say in church buildings. The finest architecture could never constitute a proper shrine for Deity. Look to the blue heavens, gaze upon the spangled vault of night, and view the ever-flashing, wide, and open sea, and tell me if any handiwork of man can rival the temple of nature. Peer into boundless space and see what a temple is already built; within what walls would you hope to house the infinite Jehovah? He has deigned, however, to choose Zion and to desire it for His habitation. The saints are built together as a spiritual house, a habitation of God through the Spirit.

God resides among His people, according to His promise, "I will dwell in them, and walk in them" (2 Cor. 6:16). Hence, the church is the home of the Great Father, where He dwells in the midst of His family and takes His rest. Has He not said, "This is my rest for ever: here will I dwell; for I have desired it" (Ps. 132:14)? As a man in his own house takes his ease and finds delight, so God takes pleasure in them that fear Him: "His foundation is in the holy mountains. The LORD loveth the gates of Zion more than all the dwellings of Jacob" (Ps. 87:1–2).

The church is God's house, for there He makes Himself known and manifests Himself as He does not to the outside world. "In Judah is God known: his name is great in Israel" (Ps. 76:1). His people know Him, for they are all taught of the Lord. None of them has need to say to his neighbor, "Know the LORD" (Jer. 31:34), for they all know Him as their Father, from the least even to the greatest. What sweet familiarities are enjoyed in the church! What holy intimacies between the great Father and His children, how tenderly does He reveal Himself so that the secret of the Lord is with them that fear Him. His saints are a people near to Him: they have access to Him at all times, for they dwell in His house and are His own dearly beloved children. What more glorious thing can be said of the church than this: "God is in the midst of her; she shall not be moved" (Ps. 46:5). Of what but the church, the true house of the Lord, could we read such words as these: "The LORD thy God in the midst of thee is mighty; he will save, he will rejoice over thee with joy; he will rest in his love, he will joy over thee with singing" (Zeph. 3:17).

The church is God's house, and therefore God provides for it even as a man cares for his own house, spending his strength for it, exercising his wisdom on its behalf, and ever being thoughtful over it. God has lain Himself down for His people. For this His Son has both died and risen again. For this the Lord arranges the purposes of heaven; for this He works among the children of men. The Lord's portion is His people. He will see to it that His spiritual house is not allowed to decay or to be short of anything that makes for its comfort, security, and honor.

The Lord links His own name with the church as a man does with his house. It is the house of the Lord, and He is the Lord of the house. It is the greatest honor that can happen to any man to be a member of the household of God. There are great houses in the world of long descent and of imperial rank, but what are they compared with the household of God? The one family in heaven and earth named by the name of Jesus has far more true glory about it than all the families of princes. I would rather be the humblest saint than the greatest emperor. Such honor have all the saints.

If you and I have had the privilege to be admitted into God's house and made a part of His family, it is exceedingly necessary that we should know the law of the house. This is desirable at our entrance and equally necessary as long as we remain in the house of the Lord. Paul wrote to Timothy with this design "that thou mayest know how thou oughtest to behave thyself in the house of God, which is the church of the living God" (1 Tim. 3:15). To this end, Ezekiel in our text was sent of God to those who desired the favor of God. He was to show them the form of the house, the goings out and the comings in thereof, all its ordinances, all its forms and laws. He was to write it in their sight that they might keep the whole form thereof, and all the ordinances thereof, and do them.

God's house is not lawless. It is the abode of liberty but not of license. They that dwell in God's house are in His immediate presence, and our God is a consuming fire (Heb. 12:29). He who dwells with the thrice holy God must be holy as well. The Lord will be sanctified in them that come near to Him, and if any enter the house to misbehave themselves, they will find that judgment begins at the house of God. How terrible are those words: "If any man defile the temple of God, him shall God destroy" (1 Cor. 3:17).

Come we, then, with great attention to look at our text that informs us as to the law of the house. Oh, that the Spirit may cause us to understand and then lead us to obey.

The Law of the House

Note the text carefully. It begins and ends with the same words: "*This is the law of the house*: Upon the top of the mountain the whole limit thereof round about shall be most holy. Behold, *this is the law of the house*." These words made a frame for the statute. Why are the words mentioned twice? Is it because we are such wayward scholars that we need to be told everything twice? Is it because we are so blind and dull that unless we have a thing repeated we are not likely to notice it, or noticing it are sure to forget it? Or was this posted up because of the peculiar law as to going in and out of the temple? When the worshiper entered, he saw over the portal, "This is the law of the house"; and when he went out, if he looked back at the gate of his departure, he would see there, too, "This is the law of the house." Or is it because this is the law of the house for the young convert, and this is the law of the house for the most venerable saint? At any rate, the alpha and omega of Christian conduct is contained in the law of the house. You can go no higher than obedience to that law. Indeed, you may say of it, "It is high, I cannot attain it." Go as far as you may, this still remains the law of the house to the most advanced among us, for the Lord's commandment is exceedingly broad.

And what is this law of the house? Why, that everything about it is *holy*. All things in the church must be pure, clean, right, gracious, commendable, Godlike. Everything that has to do with the church of God must be holy. Here are the words: "Upon the top of the mountain the whole limit round about shall be most holy." Observe that all must be *holy*; no, observe again, it must be *most holy*. In the old temple there was only one little chamber in the center that was most holy; this was called the holy of holies, or the holiness of holiness. But now in the church of God every chamber, hall, and court is to be most holy. As was the veiled shrine in which God shone forth from between the cherubim, such for holiness is the entire church to be in every member and every service.

Observe that this law of the house is not only intense, reaching to the superlative degree of holiness, but it is *most sweeping and encompassing*, for we read, "Upon the top of the mountain the whole limit thereof round about shall be most holy." The outer courts, the courts of the Gentiles, the walls, the promenades outside the walls, the slopes of the hill, every part that had to do with the mountain upon which the temple stood, was to be most holy. From which I gather that in the church of God it is not merely her ministers that are to be most holy, but all her members—not her sacraments only, but her ordinary meals; not her Sabbaths only, but her workdays; not her worship only, but her daily labor. All that surrounds our consecrated life is to be consecrated, too. The secular matters that touch our religion are to be made religious—whether we eat or drink or "whatsoever ye do in word or deed, do all in the name of the Lord Jesus" (Col. 3:17). Not only are the bells on the high priest's garments to be "holiness unto the Lord," but the bells of the horses are to be the same. The pots and bowls of our kitchens are to be as truly sacred as the golden vessels with which the priest served the altar of the Most High. Holiness should cover the whole ground of a Christian's life. The Christian should be sanctified "spirit, soul, and body," and in all things he should bear evidence of having been set apart to the Lord. Paul prayed that "the very God of peace sanctify you wholly" (1 Thess. 5:23). Amen; so let it be.

We notice that *this holiness was to be conspicuous*. The church is not as a house sequestered in a valley or hidden away in a woods. It is the temple that was set upon the top of a mountain where it could be seen from afar. The whole of that mountain was holy. Conspicuous holiness should be the mark of the church of God. We should be a peculiar people, distinguished by this as a race dwelling alone that cannot be numbered among the nations. We should be noted not for talent or wealth or loud professions but for holiness. Somehow or other true holiness is sure to be spied out and remarked upon. Like the violet, it tries to hide itself but is betrayed by its perfume. Like the star, it twinkles with modesty but is discovered by its light. Grace cannot be put under a bushel. It may desire to be sheltered from its enemies by its obscurity, but the holy city evermore stands on a hill and cannot be hid. Would to God that whenever people speak of the church to which we belong they may acknowledge its holiness! Would to God that whenever they speak of you or me they may have no evil thing to say of us unless they lie. The world does not know how to name the thing that it both admires and hates, but it soon perceives its existence and owns its power—the thing I mean is holiness, which is at once the glory and the strength of the people of God.

What is holiness? I know what it is, and yet I cannot define it in a few words. I will bring out its meaning by degrees, but I shall not do better than the poor Irish lad who had been converted to the faith. When he was asked by the missionary, "Patrick, what is holiness?" "Sir," he said, "it is having a clane inside." Just so. Morality is a clean outside, but holiness is being clean within. Morality is a dead body washed and laid in clean white linen; holiness is the living form in perfect purity. To be just to man is morality, to be hallowed unto God is holiness. The church of God must not be reputedly good, but be really pure. She must not have a name for virtue, but her heart must be right before God—she must have a clean inside. Our lives must be such that observers may peep within doors and see nothing for which to blame us. Our moral cleanliness must not be like that of a housewife who sweeps the dirt under the mats. We must be so clear of the accursed thing that even if they dig in the earth they will not find an Achan's treasure hidden there. "Behold, thou desirest truth in the inward parts: and in the hidden part thou shalt make me to know wisdom" (Ps. 51:6).

We might instructively divide holiness into four things. The first would be its negative side—*separation* from the world. There may be morality, but there can be no holiness in a worldling. The man who has experienced no change of nature and life is not yet acquainted with biblical holiness. The word to every true saint is, "Come out from among them, and be ye separate, saith the Lord, and touch not the unclean thing" (2 Cor. 6:17). If we are conformed to the world, we cannot be holy. Jesus said of all His saints, "They are not of the world, even as I am not of the world" (John 17:14). We are redeemed from among men that we may be like our Redeemer, "holy, harmless, undefiled, separate from sinners" (Heb. 7:26). We are not to be separate as to place, avoiding men with monkish fanaticism, for nobody mixed more with sinners than did our Lord. "This man receiveth sinners, and eateth with them" (Luke 15:2) is the old reproach, yet our Lord was not one of them, as everybody could see. Nothing could be more clear than the difference between the lost sheep and the Shepherd who came among them seeking out His own. Every action, every word, every movement expressed that He was a different man from the sinners whom He sought to bless. So must it be with us. As the lily among thorns so must we be among the mass of men. Are you different from those among whom you live? Are you as different from them as a Jew is from a Gentile? So it should be with the real Christian. Wherever he is and whatever he does, men should know that he is not an ordinary man. The title "the peculiar people" belongs to the followers of Jesus. They are strangers and sojourners in this world, for they have come out by the divine call to be separated unto the Lord forever. There is no holiness without separateness from the world.

Holiness next consists very largely in *consecration*. The holy things of the sanctuary were holy because they were dedicated to God. No one drank out of the sacred vessels except the priests. No victims were killed by the sacrificial knife or laid upon the altar except such as were consecrated to Jehovah, for the altar and the fire thereof was holy. So must it be with us if we are to be holy: we must belong to Jehovah, we must be consecrated to Him and be used for His own purposes. Not nominally only, but really, and as a matter of fact, we must live for God. That is our reason for existence, and if we do not answer this end, we have no excuse for living. Only so far as we are bringing glory to God are we answering the end and design of our creation. We are the Lord's priest, and if we do not serve Him we are pretenders. As Christians we are not our own but are bought with a price, and if we live as we were our own, we defraud our Redeemer. Will a man rob God? Will he rob Jesus of the purchase of His blood? Can we consent that the world, the flesh, and the devil should use the vessels that are dedicated to God? Shall such sacrilege be tolerated? No. Let us feel that we are the Lord's and that His vows are upon us, binding us to lay ourselves out for Him alone. This is an essential ingredient of holiness: the cleanest bowl in the sanctuary was not holy because it was clean. It became holy when, in addition to being cleansed, it was also hallowed unto the Lord. This is more than morality, decency, honesty, virtue. You tell me of your generosity, your goodness, and your godly intentions—what of these? Are you consecrated, for if you are not consecrated to God, you know nothing of holiness. This is the law of the house, that the church is consecrated to Christ, and that everyone who comes into her midst must be the same. We must live for God and for His glorious kingdom, or we are not holy. Oh, to make a dedication of ourselves to God without reserve and then to stand to it forever: this is the way of holiness.

But this does not complete the idea of holiness unless you add to it *conformity* to the will and character of God. If we are God's servants, we must follow God's commands, being ready to do as our Master bids us because He is the Lord. We must make the Lord Jesus our example, and as Ezekiel says, "We must measure the pattern." It must be our meat and drink to do the will of Him who sent us. Our rule is not our judgment, much less our desires, but the Word of God is our statute book. We are to obey God that we may grow like God. The question to be asked is, What would the Lord have me do? or, What would Christ Himself have done under the circumstances? Having been begotten again by God into the image of Christ, and so having become His true children, we are to grow up into Him in all things who is the head, being imitators of God as dear children, for only so shall we be holy. Do understand, then, that with regard to the whole range of the church, conformity to the character of God is the law of the house. Likeness to Christ must be seen in every single member, in every act of every member, in the whole body, and in all its corporate acts. This is the law of the house.

I must add, however, to make up the idea of holiness, that there must a close *communion* between the soul and God. If a man could be conformed to the likeness of God, yet if he never had any communication with God, the idea of holiness would not be complete. The temple becomes holy because God dwells in it. God came into the most holy place in a most special manner, and this accounted for its being the holy of holies. Even so, special communion with the Lord creates special holiness. God's presence demands and creates holiness. And so, if we would be holy, we must dwell in God and God must dwell in us. We cannot be holy at a distance from God. How is it with you? How is it with our church? Is God with us in all our services? Is He recognized with all our efforts? Does He reign in all our hearts? Does Jesus abide with us, for this is according to the law of the house that God should be everywhere recognized, that we should in all things conform to His will, in all things be consecrated to His purposes, and for His sake in all things be separated from the rest of mankind. This is the law of the house.

Let Us Examine Ourselves by This Law

The church of God is founded by a holy God upon holy principles and for holy purposes. She has been redeemed by a holy Savior with a holy sacrifice and dedicated to holy service. Her great glory is the Holy Spirit, whose influences and operations are all holy. Her law book is the holy Bible, her armory is the holy covenant, her comfort is holy prayer. Her gatherings are holy assemblies, her citizens are holy men and women, she exists for holy ends and follows after holy examples. Are you then as part of her "holiness to the Lord"? Ask yourself questions founded on what I have already said. Do I so live as to be *separated*? Is there in my business a difference between me and those with whom I work? Are my thoughts different? Does the current of my desire run in a different direction? Am I at home with the ungodly, or does their sin trouble me? Search and see whether you are holy in that sense.

Next, let each one ask, Am I *consecrated*? Am I living to God with my body, with my soul, with my spirit? Am I using my substance, my talents, my time, my voice, my thoughts for God's glory? What am I living for? Am I making a pretence to live to God and actually living for self? Am I like Ananias and Sapphira, pretending to give all and yet keeping back a part of the price?

Next ask the question, Am I living in *conformity* to the mind of the holy God? Am I living as Christ would have lived in my place? Do I as an employer, as a worker, as a husband, as a wife, or as a child act as God Himself would have me act so that He could say to me, "Well done, thou good and faithful servant"? He is a jealous God: am I obeying Him with care? If I am not walking in obedience to God, I am breaking the law of the house, and that house is the house of the living God. Should we not take heed lest we insult the King in His own palace?

Then, again, do I live in *communion* with God? I cannot be holy and yet have a wall of division between me and God. Is there a great gulf of separation between me and the Lord? Then I am a stranger to holiness. I must have fellowship with Him, or else I am living in a manner that is sinful, dangerous, grievous, injurious. Do you walk with God? Do you abide in fellowship with Jesus? I know there are some who would rather not give an answer to that question. Their nearness to God is a thing of rare occasions and not of everyday consciousness. At a meeting, when religious excitement stirs them, they are a little warmed up, but their general temperature suits the North Pole rather than the Equator. But this will not do. We want you to dwell near to God always: to wake up in the morning with His light saluting the eyes of your soul and to be with Him while you are engaged in domestic concerns or out in the busy world. We want you often to have a secret word with the

Well-beloved One during the day and to go to bed at night feeling how sweet it is to fall asleep upon the Savior's bosom. I would to God we were so encompassed with divine love, so completely sanctified, so thoroughly holy, that we never lost for an instant a sense of the immediate presence of the Most High. I leave that work of self-examination with you. Do not neglect it, for as a servant of the Lord it is incumbent upon you to remember that holiness is fitting in His house, and it will be ill for us to be walking contrary to His mind. "Measure the pattern," and measure yourself by the law of the house.

What Are the Bearings of This Law of the House?

If the church of God shall be most holy, it will have as the result of it the greatest possible degree of the smile and favor of God. A holy church has God in her midst. The consequence of God's presence is a holy liveliness in all her members, for where God comes near, lethargy and death soon fly away. Where the sacred presence abides, sickness of soul disappears. Jehovah-Rophi heals His people among whom He dwells, and the inhabitant shall no more say, "I am sick." This again causes joy, and the bones that were broken rejoice.

Where there is holiness, God comes, and there is sure to be love, for love is of the very essence of holiness. The fruit of the Spirit is love both to God and to man. That love begets union of heart, brotherly kindness, sympathy, and affection, and these bring peace and happiness. Among the truly holy there are no divisions, no heresies, no separation into parties, but all are one in Christ. When we shall be perfect as our heavenly Father is perfect, we shall love as He loves.

This, of course, leads to success in all the church's efforts, and a consequent increase. Her prayers are intense and bring down a blessing, for they are holy and acceptable to God by Jesus Christ. Her labors are abundant and secure an abundant harvest, for God will not forget her labor of love. The holy church with God in the midst of her is the place of brotherly unity, and consequently it is wet with the dew of Hermon, "and there the LORD commanded the blessing, even life for evermore" (Ps. 133:3). Saints in such a state experience foretastes of heaven. Their trials are sanctified, and their mercies are multiplied; thus faith grows exceedingly, and hope is confirmed. To their assemblies angels come trooping down and up from them, by the way of the ladder that Jacob saw. O happy people!

A holy church, may we see it! A church most holy in all her solemn services shall be "fair as the moon, clear as the sun, and terrible as an army with banners" (Song 6:10). The nations among whom she dwells shall hear the fame thereof; they shall come from afar and ask to see her prince, and they shall be astonished at His glory. The sons of the foreigners shall come bending to her feet. Her converts shall be like flocks of doves; she shall herself wonder where they have come from. There shall be no heaviness, no defeat, no disappointment, no doubt of eternal truths, and no suspicions of infinite love. In the power of the Holy Spirit, she shall be bravely confident, gloriously self-sacrificing, and so shall she go from victory to victory. Mount but this white horse of holiness, O ye armies of the Lord, and Christ shall lead the procession, and all of you clothed in fine white linen shall follow Him and go forth conquering and to conquer (Rev. 19:14).

On the other hand, imagine a church without holiness. What will come of it? Without holiness, no man shall see the Lord. And if the church cannot even see her Lord, what is her condition? Go to Zion and see what happens to God's house when once defiled. Mark how the holy and beautiful house was desolate and burnt with fire. Remember how God loathed Zion and commanded her enemies to cast her down stone from stone and sow with salt the very site on which she stood. Was there ever destruction like to what fell upon Jerusalem? Let us tolerate and indulge unholy men and women, and we shall soon see the anger of the Lord wax hot. Let us ourselves give way to laxity of principle and practice, let us lose our consecration and our communion, and what will soon be the effect? Probably first will come heartburning, envy, and strife; next, divisions, schisms, false doctrines, rivalries, contentions; or possibly the evil may take the form of lethargy, inactivity, worldliness, lack of love to Christ and souls. By and by there will be diminished gatherings at the meetings for prayer, a cessation of all earnest pleading and consecrated living; then a falling-off of congregations; then a lack of power in the ministry—a defect in the doctrine, perhaps, or else in the earnestness of the speaker; and all the while no conversions and no visitations from the Lord. Then will this church be a proverb, a byword and a hissing throughout the whole earth.

How often am I jealous about this with a burning jealousy. My heart breaks when I hear of some who live unholy lives and so walk as to dishonor the cross of Christ. I mean not such as we can lay our finger on and say, "This man is a drunkard, or unchaste, or dishonest," else, as you well know, church discipline would be applied. But I mean such as cannot be thus dealt with because their sins are not open—the tares that grow up in the wheat, the actions not yet discovered (Matt. 13:25). I tremble lest there should be among us some, utterly unknown to us and undiscoverable by the most vigilant eye, whose sin, nevertheless, like a leprosy, should eat into the house and make it unfit for the habitation of God. Oh, that we may never be so fallen that God Himself shall say, "Let them alone." It was an awful moment when, in the holy place at Jerusalem, there was heard the moving of wings and a voice that said, "Let us go hence" (John 14:31). Then the glory will have departed. Woe, woe, woe! Let the curtain drop with a shower of tears upon it. God grant it never may be so!

Let Us Secure Obedience to the Law of the House

I believe that Jesus is always working in His own way for the purity of every true church. "Whose fan is in his hand"—see it moving continually—"and he will thoroughly purge his floor" (Luke 3:17). God's melting fire is not in the world where the dross contains no gold, but "whose fire is in Zion, and his furnace in Jerusalem" (Isa. 31:9). "The LORD will judge his people" (Ps. 135:14). The Lord tries professing believers and their professions. I believe that there is a judgment going on over church members that some are little aware of. Paul speaks of a church in his day in this manner, noting their inconsistencies and adding, "For this cause many are weak and sickly among you, and many sleep" (1 Cor. 11:30). A special jurisdiction is over the palace of a king. Church members are under peculiar discipline, as it is written, "You only have I known of all the families of the earth: therefore I will punish you for all your iniquities" (Amos 3:2).

Our Lord Jesus often makes the ministry to be as a great win-
nowing fan. Somebody is offended and leaves. What a mercy! You
could not have compelled him to depart, but He removes of His
own accord, and so the house is cleansed. The breath of the Spirit
blows away much chaff. When our Lord preached His usual doctrine, the chaff kept with the wheat, but when He came to speak
of eating His flesh and drinking His blood, the baser sort were
offended and "walked no more with him" (John 6:66). Did He
grieve over that separation between the precious and the vile? I do
not think so. He meant it should be so. A certain truth put in a
certain way, with a personally pointed application, perhaps not
intended by the preacher as to that particular individual, is nevertheless intended by God for that person, and the cutting word
removes the rotten bough. Thus the purging work proceeds from
day to day. We may expect our Master to come among us with a
scourge of small cords and cleanse the temple of God lest it should
become a den of thieves (Matt. 21:12–13). He is a jealous God, and
He will not allow defilement among His own people.

Have you never seen great Christian communities at a certain
phase of their existence come into troubled waters and break up
like wrecks? There must have been a secret reason; probably the
one assigned at the time was by no means the true one. Lack of
holiness led to lack of love, and unloving spirits soon found a pre-
text for dispute. Those who should have met this with love and
quenched it by gentle wisdom acted in a harsh spirit, being themselves deficient in grace, and so flint met steel and sparks
abounded. The open mischief was an effect rather than a cause,
and it may be hoped was even part of the cure. True, many a table
of the moneychangers was upset, and many a dove was seen to fly
away in fright, but the scourge did not fail to make a clearance.
How much better would it have been had there been no need for
such a purging. If churches are not holy, they cannot be prosperous,
for God afflicts those who break the law of His house.

Cannot we give earnest heed that this law is upheld among us?
"Yes," say you, "take care that you who are pastors, elders, and
deacons are watchful and faithful. Guard well the door of the
church, and see to it that you do not admit the ungodly. Be vigilant
also in discipline, so that when any are manifestly unholy they are

put away." Brethren, this is hopefully their desire and labor, but after all, what can they do? With all diligence what can a small band of officers accomplish in a church that may be numbered by hundreds or thousands? Let every man bear his own burdens. I would have every man sweep in front of his own door. I pray that each person may be jealous for purity and watch over both himself and his brethren lest any form of sin should be a root of bitterness to trouble us and thereby many should be defiled.

Let us set to this work at once. Here is the first exercise for us: let us *repent of past failures* in holiness. We shall never overcome sin till we are conscious of it and ashamed of it. Hence the Lord said to the prophet, "Thou son of man, shew the house to the house of Israel, that they may be ashamed of their iniquities: and let them measure the pattern. And if they be ashamed of all that they have done, shew them the form of the house, and the fashion thereof" (Ezek. 43:10–11). The first step toward purity is penitence. Let us bow our heads and lament before the Lord the sins of our holy things, our personal trespasses, our transgressions against love, our offences against the law of the house. He that is least ashamed will probably be the person who has most cause to blush, and he who will be most humbled will be the man who has least transgressed. In any case, we have sinned as a church and come short of the glory of God, and an honest confession is due from us.

Having owned our error, let us next *make the law of God's house our earnest study* that we may avoid offenses in the future. You will hardly keep the law if you do not know it. Search the sacred Word day and night. Let the inspired page be your standard. Never mind what others tell you; observe what the Spirit of God tells you. Get to your Bibles, search them, and there see how you should behave in the house of God. Be much upon your knees asking the Lord to teach you His mind and will, and especially beseech Him to write His law upon your hearts, for you will never keep it in your life until it is written there.

When you have studied the law of the house, then next *be intensely real in your endeavor to observe it.* How much of the religion of the present day is a sham. Men talk of being holy, but do they know what they mean? We speak of consecration, and yet we live as if we were mere worldlings hunting for wealth, fame, or pleasure. Some sing of giving all to God, and yet their contributions are miserably small. Some say they are living wholly for God, but if they had lived wholly for themselves it would not have made any particular difference in what they have done. Let us be real! Do not let us preach what we do not believe or profess to be believers in a creed that is not true to our own souls. Get a grip of eternal things; hold them, feel their solemn weight, and live under their influence. That which is unreal is unholy. The bloated Pharisee is unholy; the empty formalist in unholy; but the sincere penitent, the truly honest seeker after holiness is already holy in some degree. Your eyes, O Lord, are upon truth.

Then *let us cry for a sincere and growing faith* in God concerning this matter of holiness. Let us believe in Jesus, that by His Holy Spirit He can make us holy. Do not let us believe that any sin is inevitable; rather let us feel bound to overcome it. Let us not trust in our own struggles and strivings, but let us as much trust Christ to work in us sanctification as to work for us justification. Let faith deal with the water as well as with the blood, for they both flowed from the same fountain in the Savior's riven side.

And lastly let us *pray to be set on fire with an intense zeal for God.* I do not believe that there is such a thing as cold holiness in the world. As soon as a bullock was dedicated to God and brought to the altar, it had to be burned with fire, and so must every consecrated life. You and I are never the Lord's while we are coldhearted. We must be on fire if we are to be sacrifices acceptable to God by Jesus Christ. Oh, to be baptized into the Holy Ghost and into fire. Refining fire go through and through our souls till all that defiles shall be utterly consumed and we shall be as ingots of pure gold, wholly the Lord's.

Would any of you, Paul asks, cast a slur on the cross—you who have been converted—you before whose eyes Jesus Christ has been openly set forth as crucified (Gal. 3:1)? How his eyes flash; how his lips quiver; how his heart grows hot within him; with what vehemence he protests: "God forbid that I should glory, save in the cross of our Lord Jesus Christ." Paul spreads his eagle wing and rises into eloquence at once, while still his keen eye looks fiercely upon every enemy of the cross whom he leaves far beneath. Often in his epistles you observe this. He burns, he glows, he mounts, he soars, he is carried clean away as soon as his thoughts are in fellowship with his Lord Jesus, that meek and patient Sufferer, who offered Himself a sacrifice for our sins. When his tongue begins to speak of the glorious work that the Christ of God has done for the sons of men, it finds a sudden liberty. May we have something of that glow within our breast whenever we think of our Lord. God forbid that we should be coldhearted when we come near to Jesus. God forbid that we should ever view with heartless eye and lethargic soul the sweet wonders of that cross on which our Savior loved and died.

Chapter Eight

Three Crosses

But God forbid that I should glory, save in the cross of our Lord Jesus Christ, by whom the world is crucified unto me, and I unto the world—Galatians 6:14.

WHENEVER WE REBUKE OTHER PEOPLE, we should be prepared to clear ourselves of their offense. The Apostle Paul had been rebuking those who wished to glory in the flesh. In denouncing the false teachers and their deceived followers, he used strong language while appealing to plain facts and maintaining his ground with solid arguments. This he did without fear of being met by a counterpoint that would weaken his position. He confronts them straight on when he contrasts his own determined purpose with their plausible falseness. They were for making a good showing in the flesh, but he refused to shrink back from the deepest shame of the Christian profession. So far from shrinking, he even counted it an honor to be scorned for Christ's sake, exclaiming, "God forbid that I should glory, save in the cross of our Lord Jesus Christ." The Galatians, and all others to whom Paul's name was familiar, well knew how truly he spoke, for the manner of his life as well as the matter of his teaching had supplied evidence of this assertion, which none of his enemies could deny. There had not been in all his ministry any doctrine that Paul extolled more highly than this of "Christ crucified" (1 Cor. 1:23), nor any experience that he touched on more tenderly than this fellowship with Christ "of his sufferings" (Phil. 3:10), nor any rule of conduct that he counted more safe than this following in the footsteps of Him who "endured the cross, despising the shame, and is set down at the right hand of the throne of God" (Heb. 12:2). Paul's life was a constant testimony to this precept.

God grant, of His grace, that we might possess this same transparent consistency. Sometimes when we notice an evil and protest as boldly and conscientiously as we can against it, we feel that our protest is too obscure to have much influence. It will then be our very best resources to resolutely abstain from the evil ourselves and so, at least in one person, to overthrow its power. If you cannot convert a man from his error by an argument, you can at least prove the sincerity of your reasoning by your own behavior. If no fortress is captured, you will at least "hold the fort," and you may do more: your faithfulness may win more than your zeal. Vow faithfully within your own heart and say frankly to your neighbor, "You may do what you will; but as for me, God forbid that I seek out new paths, however inviting, or turn aside from that which I know to be the good way." A determined resolution of that sort, fully adhered to, will often carry more weight and exert more influence on the mind of an individual than a host of arguments. Your actions will speak louder than your words.

The apostle in the present case is moved with emotion at the thought of anybody presuming to set a carnal ordinance in front of the cross, by wishing to glory in circumcision or any other outward institution. The idea of a ceremony claiming to be made more of than faith in Jesus provoked Paul, till his heart presently grew hot with indignation, and he thundered forth the words, "God forbid!" He never used the sacred name with lightness, but when the fire was hot within him, he called God to witness that he did not and could not glory in anything but the cross. Indeed, there is to every true-hearted believer something shocking and revolting in the putting of anything before Jesus Christ, be it what it may, whether it is an idol or superstition or a toy of skepticism, whether it is the fruit of tradition or the flower of philosophy. Do you want new Scriptures to supplement the true sayings of God? Do you want a new Savior who can surpass Him whom the Father has sealed? Do you want a new sacrifice that can save you from sin that His atoning blood could not forgive? Do you want a modern song to supersede the new song of "worthy is the Lamb that was slain"?

"O foolish Galatians!" said Paul (Gal. 3:1). "O silly Protestants!" I am inclined to say. We might go on in these times to speak warmly to many of the parties around us. I only wish that some who think so little of doctrinal discrepancies, as they call them, could but sympathize a little with Paul's holy indignation when he saw the first symptoms of departure from godly simplicity and sincerity. Do you notice that Peter's little hypocrisy caused Paul to withstand him to his face (Gal. 2:11)? When a whole company turned the cold shoulder to the cross of Christ, it made Paul burn with indignation (Gal. 2:14). He could not stand it. The cross was the center of his hopes; around it his affection twined; there he had found peace for his troubled conscience. God forbid that he should allow it to be trampled on. Besides, it was the theme of his ministry. "Christ crucified" had already proved the power of God to salvation to every soul who had believed the lifegiving message as he proclaimed it in every city.

Would any of you, Paul asks, cast a slur on the cross—you who have been converted—you before whose eyes Jesus Christ has been openly set forth as crucified (Gal. 3:1)? How his eyes flash; how his lips quiver; how his heart grows hot within him; with what vehemence he protests: "God forbid that I should glory, save in the cross of our Lord Jesus Christ." Paul spreads his eagle wing and rises into eloquence at once, while still his keen eye looks fiercely upon every enemy of the cross whom he leaves far beneath. Often in his epistles you observe this. He burns, he glows, he mounts, he soars, he is carried clean away as soon as his thoughts are in fellowship with his Lord Jesus, that meek and patient Sufferer, who offered Himself a sacrifice for our sins. When his tongue begins to speak of the glorious work that the Christ of God has done for the sons of men, it finds a sudden liberty. May we have something of that glow within our breast whenever we think of our Lord. God forbid that we should be coldhearted when we come near to Jesus. God forbid that we should ever view with heartless eye and lethargic soul the sweet wonders of that cross on which our Savior loved and died.

Let us, then, in that spirit approach our text. We notice at once three crucifixions. "God forbid that I should glory, save in the cross of our Lord Jesus Christ"—that is, *Christ crucified*. "By whom" or "by which" (read it whichever way you like) "the world is crucified unto me"—that is *a crucified world*. "And I unto the world"—that is, *Paul himself, or the believer, crucified with Christ*. I see, again, Calvary before me with its three crosses—Christ in the center and on either side of Him a crucified person: one who dies to feel the second death and another who dies to be with Him in paradise.

Christ Crucified

I call your attention to the language: "God forbid that I should glory, save in the cross." Some popular authors and public speakers, when they have to state a truth, count it necessary to clothe it in very delicate language. They perhaps do not quite intend to conceal its point and edge; but at any rate, they do not want the projecting angles and bare surfaces of the truth to be too observable. As they cast a cloak around it, they are actually sheathing the sword of the Spirit. The Apostle Paul might have done so here, if he had chosen, but he disdains the device. He presents the truth "in the worst possible form," as his opponents say—"in all its naked hideousness," as the Jew would have it. He does not say, "God forbid that I should glory, save in the *death* of Christ," but in the *cross*. We do not realize how the use of that word *cross* would grate on ears refined in Galatia and elsewhere. In those days it meant the criminal's tree, the hangman's gibbet. We have become so accustomed to associate the name of "the cross" with other sentiments that it does not convey to us that sense of disgrace that it would inflict upon those who heard Paul speak. A family sensitively shrinks if one of its members has been hanged, and much the same would be the natural feeling of one who was told that his leader was crucified. Paul lets the phrase jar his listeners harshly, though it may prove to some a stumbling block and to others foolishness. But he will not cloak it; he glories in *the cross*!

On the other hand, I earnestly entreat you to observe how he seems to contrast the glory of the person with the shame of the suffering. It is not simply the death of Christ, nor of Jesus, nor of

Jesus Christ, nor of *the* Lord Jesus Christ, but of *our Lord Jesus Christ.* Every word tends to set forth the excellence of His person, the majesty of His character, and the interest that all the saints have in Him. It *was* a cross, but it was the cross of our Lord: let us worship Him! It was the cross of our Lord Jesus the Savior: let us love Him! It was the cross of our Jesus Christ the anointed Messiah: let us reverence Him! Let us sit at His feet and learn of Him! Each one may say, "It was the cross of *my* Lord Jesus Christ. But it sweetens the whole matter and gives a largeness to it when we say, "It was the cross of *our* Lord Jesus Christ." Oh yes, we delight to think of the contrast between the precious Christ and the painful cross, the Son of God and the shameful gibbet. He was Immanuel, God with us. Yet He died the criminal's death upon the accursed tree. Paul brings out the shame with great sharpness and the glory with great plainness. He does not hesitate in either case, whether he would declare the sufferings of Christ or the glory that should follow.

What does Paul mean, however, by the cross? Of course he cared nothing for the particular piece of wood to which those blessed hands and feet were nailed, for that was mere materialism. The apostle means the glorious doctrine of justification—free justification—through the atoning sacrifice of Jesus Christ. This is what he means by the cross—the expiation for sin that our Lord Jesus Christ made by His death and the gift of eternal life freely bestowed on all those who by grace are led to trust in Him. To Paul the cross meant just what the brazen serpent meant to Moses (Num. 21:6–9). As the brazen serpent in the wilderness was the hope of the sin-bitten, and all that Moses had to do was bid them look and live, so today the cross of Christ—the atonement of Jesus Christ—is the hope of mankind, and our mission is continually to cry, "Look and live! Look and live!" It is this doctrine—this gospel of Christ crucified—at which the present age, with all its vaunted culture and all its vain philosophies, sneers so broadly. It is this doctrine wherein we glory. We are not ashamed to put it very definitely: we glory in substitution, in the vicarious sacrifice of Jesus in our stead. He was "made to be sin for us, who knew no sin; that we might be made the righteousness of God in him" (2 Cor. 5:21). "All we like sheep have gone astray; we have turned every one to his own way; and the LORD hath laid on him the iniquity of us all" (Isa. 53:6). "Christ hath redeemed us from the curse of the law, being made a curse for us: for it is written, Cursed is every one that hangeth on a tree" (Gal. 3:13). We believe in the imputation of sin to the innocent person of our covenant Head and Representative, in the bearing of the penalty by that substituted One and the clearing by faith of those for whom He bore the punishment of sin.

Now we glory in this. We glory in it, not as men sometimes boast in a creed that they have received by tradition from their forefathers, for we have learned this truth—each one for himself—by the inward teaching of the Holy Spirit, and therefore it is very dear to us. We glory in it with no empty boast but to the inward satisfaction of our own hearts. We prove that satisfaction by the devout consecration of our lives to make it known. We have trusted our souls to its truth. If it is a fable, our hopes are forever shipwrecked, for our all is embarked in that venture. We are quite prepared to run that risk, content to perish if this salvation should fail us. We live upon this faith. Take this away and there is nothing left us in the Bible worth the having. It has become to us the beginning and end of our confidence, our hope, our rest, our joy. Instead of being ashamed to preach it, we wish that we could stand somewhere where all the inhabitants of the earth should hear us, and we would thunder it out day and night. So far from being ashamed of acknowledging it, we count it to be our highest honor and our greatest delight to tell it abroad, as we have opportunity, among the sons of men.

But why do we rejoice in it? Why do we glory in it? The answer is so large that I cannot do more than glance at its manifold claims on our gratitude. We glory in it for a thousand reasons. We fail to see anything in the doctrine of atonement that we should not glory in. We have heard a great many dogs bark against it, but dogs will bay at the moon in her brightness, and therefore we mind not their howlings. Their noise has sometimes disturbed, though never yet has it frightened us. We have not yet heard a cavil against our Lord or an argument against His atoning blood that has affected our faith. The Scriptures affirm it, the Holy Spirit bears witness to it, and its effect upon our inner life assures us of it. It lightens our conscience, gladdens our hearts, inspires our devotion, and elevates our aspirations. We are wedded to it and daily glory in it.

In the cross of Christ we glory because we regard it as a matchless exhibition of the attributes of God. We see there the love of

God desiring a way by which He might save mankind, aided by His wisdom, so that a plan is perfected by which the deed can be done without violation of truth and justice. In the cross we see a strange conjunction of what once appeared to be two opposite qualities: justice and mercy. We see how God is supremely just, as just as if He had no mercy and yet infinitely merciful in the gift of His son. Mercy and justice in fact become counsel upon the same side and irresistibly plead for the acquittal of the believing sinner. We can never tell which of these two attributes of God shines more glorious in the sacrifice of Christ. They both find a glorious high throne in the person and work of the Lamb of God that takes away the sin of the world. Since it has become, as it were, the mirror that reflects the character and perfections of God, it is only right that we should glory in the cross of Christ.

We glory in the cross as the manifestation of the love of Jesus. He was loving inasmuch as He came to earth at all—loving in feeding the hungry, in healing the sick, in raising the dead. He was loving in His whole life. He was embodied charity, the Prince of philanthropists, the King of kindly souls. But oh, His death!—His cruel and shameful death—bearing, as we believe He did, the wrath due to sin, subjecting Himself to the curse, though in Him was no sin. This shows the love of Christ at its highest altitude, and therefore do we glory in it and will never be ashamed to do so.

We glory in the cross because it is the putting away of sin. There was no other way of making an end of sin and making reconciliation for iniquity. To forgive the transgressions without exacting the penalty would have been contrary to all the threatenings of God. It would not have appeased the claims of justice nor satisfied the conscience of the sinner. No peace of mind can be enjoyed without pardon, and conscience declares that no pardon can be obtained without an atonement. We would have to live with the fear that it was only a reprieve and not a remission, even if the most comforting promise had been given unsealed with the atoning blood. The instincts of nature have convinced men of this truth, for all the world over, religion has been associated with sacrifice. Almost every kind of worship that has ever sprung up among the sons of men has had sacrifice for its most prominent feature. Crime must be avenged, evil and sin cry from the ground, and a victim is sought to avert the vengeance. The heart craves for something that can calm the conscience. Christ did make His soul an offering for sin, when His "own self bare our sins in His own body on the tree" (1 Pet. 2:24). With His expiring breath He said, "It is finished!" Oh, wondrous grace! Pardon is now freely published among the sons of men, pardon of which we see the justice and validity. As far as the east is from the west, so far has God removed our transgressions from us by the death of Christ. This and this alone will put away sin, therefore in this cross of Christ we glory. Yes, and in it alone will we glory ever more.

The cross of Christ has put away our sins, blessed be God, so that this load and burden of sin no more weigh us down! We do not speak at random now. The cross has breathed hope and peace and joy into our spirits. I am sure that no one knows how to glory in the cross unless he has experienced its peace-breathing power. I speak what I do know and testify what I have felt. The burden of sin lay so heavy upon me that I would sooner have died than lived. Many days and nights I felt the flames of hell in the anguish of my heart because I knew my guilt but saw no way of righteous forgiveness. Yet in a moment the load was lifted from me, and I felt overflowing love to the Savior. I fell at His feet awestruck that He should have ever taken away my sin and made an end of it. That matchless deed of love won my heart to Jesus. He changed my nature and renewed my soul in that same hour. But, oh, the joy I had! Those who have sunk to the very depths of despair and risen in a moment to the heights of peace and joy unspeakable can tell you that they must glory in the cross and its power to save.

We cannot misrepresent that inward witness. We only wish that others had been as deeply convinced of sin and led to the cross to feel their burden roll off their shoulder as we have been, and then they, too, would glory in the cross of Christ. We have gone with this remedy in our hands to souls that have been near despair, and we have never found the medicine to fail. Many times I have spoken to people so depressed in spirit that they seemed not far from insanity, so heavy was their sense of sin. Yet I have never known the matchless music of Jesus' name in any case to fail to charm the soul out of its despondency. "They looked unto him, and were lightened: and their faces were not ashamed" (Ps. 34:5). Men who, because they thought there was no hope for them, would have desperately continued in sin have read that word *hope* written in crimson lines upon the Savior's dying body, and they have sprung up into confidence, have entered into peace, and henceforth have begun to lead a new life. We glory in the cross because of the peace it brings to every troubled conscience that receives it by faith. Our own case has proved to our own souls its efficacy, and what we have seen in others has confirmed our confidence.

Yet we should not glory so much in the cross were we not convinced that it is the greatest moral power in all the world. We glory in the cross because it gets at men's hearts when nothing else can reach them. The story of the dying Savior's love has often impressed those whom all the moral lectures in the world could never have moved. Judged and condemned by the unanswerable reasonings of their own consciences, they have not had control enough over their passions to shake off the captivity in which they were held by the temptations that assailed them at every turn, till they have drawn near to the cross of Jesus and from pardon have gathered hope and from hope have gained strength to master sin. When they have seen their sin laid on Jesus, they have loved Him and hated the sin that made Him suffer so grievously as their substitute. Then the Holy Spirit has come upon them, and they have resolved with divine strength to drive out the sin for which the Savior died. They have begun a new life, and they have continued in it. Sustained by the same sacred power that first constrained them, they now look forward to be perfected by it through the power of God. Where are the triumphs of unbelievers in rescuing men from sin? Where are the trophies of philosophy in conquering human pride? Will you bring us harlots that have been made chaste, thieves that have been reclaimed, angry men of bearlike temper who have become harmless as lambs, through scientific lectures? Let our amateur philanthropists, who suggest so much and do so little, produce some instances of the moral transformations that have been wrought by their sophistries. It is the cross that humbles the proud, lifts up the fallen, refines the polluted, and gives a fresh start to those who are forlorn and desperate. Nothing else can do it. The world sinks lower and lower into the bog of its own selfishness and sin. Only this wondrous lever of the atonement, symbolized by the cross of Christ, can lift our abject race to the place of virtue and honor that it should occupy.

We glory in the cross for so many reasons that I cannot hope to enumerate them all. While it ennobles our life, it invigorates us with hope in our death. Death is now deprived of its terrors to us, for Christ has died. We, like Him, can say, "Father, into thy hands I commend my spirit" (Luke 23:46). His burial has perfumed the grace; His resurrection has paved the road to immortality. He rose and left a lamp behind that shows an outlet from the gloom of the sepulcher. The paradise He immediately predicted for Himself and for the penitent thief who hung by His side has shown us how quick the transition is from mortal pains to immortal joys. "Absent from the body, present with the Lord," is the blessed prospect. Glory be to Christ forever and ever that we have this doctrine of "Christ crucified" to preach.

The World Crucified

The apostle said that the world was crucified to him. What does he mean by this? He regarded the world as nailed up like a criminal and hanged upon a cross to die. I suppose he means that its character was condemned. Paul looked out upon the world that thought so much of itself and said, "I do not think much of you, poor world! You are like a doomed felon." He knew that the world had crucified its Savior—crucified its God. It had gone to such a length of sin that it had hounded perfect innocence through the streets. Infinite benevolence it had scoffed at and maligned. Eternal truth it had rejected and preferred a lie, and the Son of God, who was love incarnate, it had put to the death of the cross. "Now," says Paul, "I know your character, O world! I know you and hold you in no more esteem than the wretch abhorred for his crimes who is condemned to hang upon the cross and so end his detested life." This led Paul, since he condemned its character, utterly to despise its judgment. The world said, "This Paul is a fool. His gospel is foolishness and he himself is a mere babbler." "Yes," thought Paul, "a great deal you know of it!" In this we unite with Paul and say, "What is your judgment worth? You did not know the Son of God, poor blind world! We are sure that He was perfect, and yet you hunted Him to death. Your judgment is a poor thing, O world! You are crucified to us."

There are many people who can hardly stand to live if they

happen to be misjudged by the world or what is called "society." Oh yes, they say, we must be respectable. We must have every man's good word or we are ready to faint. Paul was of another mind. What did he care what the world might say? How could he wish to please a world so abominable that it had put his Lord to death! He would sooner have its bad opinion than its good. Better to be frowned at than to be smiled upon by a world that crucified Christ. Certainly, its condemnation is more worth having than its approval if it can put Christ to death. Paul utterly despised the world's judgment, and the world was crucified to him.

Today we are told to think a great deal about "public opinion," "popular belief," and "the sentiment of the period." I should like to see how Paul would look after he had read some of those expressions about the necessity of keeping ourselves abreast with the sentiment of the period. "What!" he would say. "The sentiment of the world! It is crucified to me! What can it matter what its opinion is? We are of God, little children, and the whole world lies in the wicked one. Would you heed what the world thinks of you or of the truth of your Lord? Are you going to smooth your tongue and soften your speech to please the world that lies in the wicked one!" Paul would be indignant with such a proposition. He said, "the world is crucified to me." Hence, he looked upon all the world's pleasures as so much rottenness, a carcass nailed to a cross. Can you imagine Paul being taken to the Colosseum at Rome, being made to sit on one of those benches to watch a combat of gladiators. There is the emperor and all the great peers of Rome and the senators. There are those cruel eyes all gazing down upon men who shed each other's blood. Can you picture how Paul would have felt if he had been forced to occupy a seat at that spectacle? He would have closed his eyes and ears against the sight of what Rome thought to be the choicest pleasure of the day. That was the world of Paul's day, and Paul rightly judged it to be a crucified felon. If he were compelled to see the popular pleasures of today, would he not be as sick of them as he would have been of the amusements of Rome?

To Paul, too, all the honors of the age must have been crucified in like manner. Suppose that Paul settled his mind to think of the wretches who were reigning as emperors in his day! I use the word carefully, for I would not speak evil of dignities. But really I speak too well of them when I call them wretches. They seem to have been inhuman monsters to whom every kind of lust was a daily habit and who even sought out new inventions of sensuality, calling them new pleasures. As Paul thought of the iniquities of Napoli and all the great towns to which the Romans went in their holidays—Pompeii and the like—oh, how he loathed them!

Alike contemptuously did Paul judge of all the treasures of the world. Paul never spent as much time as it would take to wink his eye in thinking of how much money he was worth. Having food and clothing, he was content. Sometimes he had scarcely that. He casually thanks the Philippians for ministering to his necessities, but he never sought to store anything, nor did he live with even half a thought of aggrandizing himself with gold and silver (Phil. 4:10). "No," he said, "this will all perish with the using," and so he treated the world as a thing crucified to him. Can you say as much as this—that the world in its materialism as well as in its motley vices and its manifold trivialities is a crucified thing to you? Here's what the world says: "Make money, young man, make money! Honestly if you can, but by all means make money. Look about you, for if you are not sharp you will not succeed. Keep your own counsel and play your cards well." Now, suppose that you get the money. What is the result? The net result, as I often find it, is a paragraph in one of newspapers to say that So-and-so's will was proved in the probate court under so many thousands. Then follows a squabble among all his relatives. That is the consummation of a life of toil and care and scheming. He has lived for money, and he has to leave it behind. There is the end of that folly.

I have sometimes thought of the contrast between the poor man's funeral and the rich man's funeral. When the poor man dies, there are his sons and daughters weeping with real distress, for the death of the father brings sadness and sympathy into that house. The poor man is to be buried, but it can be managed only as all the children pinch themselves to pay a little. They *do* suffer, and they prove their sorrow by rivalling one another in the respect they pay to their parent. Now you shall see the rich man die. Of course, everybody laments the sad loss: it is the proper thing. Empty carriages swell the procession to the grave by way of empty compliment. The mourners return, and there is the reading of that blessed document the will. When the will is read, the time for tears is over in almost every case. Few are pleased; the one whom fortune favors is the envy of all the rest. Sad thoughts and sullen looks float on the surface, not in respect of the man's departure, but concerning the *means* he has left and the mode in which he has disposed of them.

It is a poor thing to live for the making of money and the hoarding of it. But still the genius of rightly getting money can be consecrated to the glory of God. You can use the wealth of this world in the service of the Master. To gain is not wrong. It is wrong only when grasping becomes the main object of life and grudging grows into covetousness, which is idolatry. To every believer, that love and every other form of worldliness should be crucified so that we can say, "For me to live is not myself, but it is Christ. I love that I may honor and glorify Him."

When the apostle said that the world was crucified to him, he meant just this. "I am not enslaved by any of its pursuits. I care nothing for its maxims. I am not governed by its spirit. I do not court its smiles. I do not fear its threatenings. It is not my master nor am I its slave." The whole world cannot force Paul to lie or to sin, but Paul will tell the world the truth, come what may. Recollect the words of Palissy, the potter, when the king of France said to him that if he did not change his religion and cease to be a Huguenot, he was afraid that he should have to deliver him up to his enemies. "Sire," said the potter, "I am sorry to hear you say, 'I am afraid,' for all the men in the world could not make Palissy talk like that. I am afraid of nobody, and I *must* do nothing but what is right." The man who fears God and loves the cross has a moral backbone that enables him to stand, and he snaps his fingers at the world. "Dead felon!" says he. "Dead felon! Crucifier of Christ! *Cosmos* you call yourself. By beautiful names you would desire to be greeted. Paul is nothing in your esteem, but Paul is a match for you, for he thinks as much of you as you do of him, and no more." Hear him as he cries, "The world is crucified unto me, and I unto the world." To live to serve men is one thing, to live to bless them is another; and this we will do, God helping us, making sacrifices for their good. But to fear men, to ask their permission to think, to ask their instructions as to what we shall speak and how we shall say it—that is an evil we cannot tolerate. By the grace of God, we have not so degraded ourselves and never shall. "The world is crucified to me," says the apostle, "by the cross of Christ."

I Am Crucified to the World

We soon see the evidence of this crucifixion if we notice how they poured contempt upon Paul. Once Saul was a great rabbi, a man profoundly versed in Hebrew lore, a Pharisee of the Pharisees, and much admired. He was also a classic scholar and a philosophic thinker, a man of great mental powers, and he was prepared to take the lead in learned circles. But when Paul began to preach Christ crucified—"Bah," they said, "he is an utter fool! Do not listen to him!" Or else they said, "Down with him! He is an apostate!" They cursed him. His name brought wrath into the face of all Jews that mentioned it, and all intelligent Greeks likewise. "Paul? He is a nobody!" He was everybody when he thought their way; he is a nobody now that he thinks God's way.

And then they put him to open shame by suspecting all his motives and by misrepresenting all his actions. It did not matter what Paul did. They were quite certain that he was self-seeking, that he was endeavoring to make a fine thing of it for himself. When he acted so that they were forced to admit that he was right, they put it in such a light that they made it out to be wrong. There were some who denied his apostleship and said that he was never sent of God; others questioned his ability to preach the gospel. So they crucified poor Paul one way and another to the full.

They went further still. They despised, they shunned him. His old friends forsook him. Some got out of the way, others pointed at him the finger of scorn in the streets. His persecutors showed their rancor against him, stoning him with lynch law and then with a semblance of legality dragging him before the magistrates. Paul was crucified to them. As for his teaching, they decried him as a babbler—one who set forth strange gods. I dare say they often sneered at the cross of Christ that he preached as a nine-days' wonder, an almost exploded doctrine, and said, "If you do but shut the mouths of men such as Paul, it will soon be forgotten." I have heard them say in modern times to lesser men, "Your old-fashioned Puritanism is nearly dead. Before long it will be utterly extinct!" But we preach Christ crucified, the same doctrine as the apostles preached, and for this by the contempt of the worldly wise we are crucified.

If you keep to the cross of Christ, you must expect to have this for your portion. The world will be crucified to you, and you will be crucified to the world. You will get the cold shoulder. Old friends will become open foes. They will begin to hate you more than they loved you before. At home your foes will be the men of your own household. You will hardly be able to do anything right. When you joined in their revelry, you were a fine fellow; when you could drink and sing a lascivious song, you were a good fellow. But now they rate you as a fool. They call you a hypocrite and slanderously blacken your character. Let their dislike be a badge of your discipleship and say, "Now also the world is crucified to me, and I to the world. Whatever the world says against me for Christ's sake is the ramblings of a doomed convict, and what do I care for that. On the other hand, if I am rejected and despised, I am only taking what I always expected—my crucifixion—in my poor, humble way after the manner of Christ Himself, who was despised and rejected of men."

The moral and the lesson of it all is this. Whatever comes of it, still glory in Christ. Whether you are in honor or in dishonor, in good report or in evil report, whether God multiplies your substance and makes you rich or diminishes it and makes you poor, you will still glory in the cross of Christ. If you have health and strength and vigor to work for Him, or if you have to lie upon a bed of languishing and bear in patience all your heavenly Father's will, resolve that you will still glory in the cross. Let this be the point of your glorifying throughout your life. Go down the steeps of Jordan, and go through Jordan itself, still glorying in the cross, for in the heaven of glory you will find that the blood-bought hosts celebrate the cross as the trophy of their redemption.

Are you trusting in the cross? Are your resting in Jesus? If not, may the Lord teach you this blessed privilege. There is no joy like it. There is no strength like it. There is no life like it. There is no peace like it. At the cross we find our heaven. It is through the cross that all heavenly, holy things abound within our hearts. If you have never been there, may the Lord lead you there at this moment to partake of His grace.

One of the best tests of a man's character will be found in his deepest and heartiest longings. You cannot always judge a man by what he is doing at any one time, for he may be under constraints that compel him to act contrary to his true self, or he may be under a temporary impulse from which he will soon be free. He may for a while be held back from that which is evil, and yet he may be radically bad; or he may be constrained by force of temptation to that which is wrong, and yet his real self may rejoice in righteousness. A man may not certainly be pronounced to be good because for the moment he is doing good, nor may he be condemned as evil because under certain constraints he may be committing sin. A man's longings are more inward and more near to his real self than his outward acts; they are more natural in that they are entirely free and beyond compulsion or restraint. As a man longeth in his heart, so is he. I do not mean every idle wish, but I refer to the strong desires of the heart. These are the lifeblood of a man's nature. You can know whether you yourself are good or evil by answering the question, To which do you have the greatest desire? Do you continually long after selfish pleasures? Then you are evil, beyond all question. Do you sigh to be and do that which is good—is this the great aim of your life? Then in the core of your being there is some good thing toward the Lord God of Israel. Your heart-longings may furnish you with excellent helps for self-examination, and I beg you to apply them at once. The things of the heart touch the root of the matter.

Chapter Nine

Holy Longings

My soul breaketh for the longing that it hath unto thy judgments at all times—Psalm 119:20.

ONE OF THE BEST TESTS of a man's character will be found in his deepest and heartiest longings. You cannot always judge a man by what he is doing at any one time, for he may be under constraints that compel him to act contrary to his true self, or he may be under a temporary impulse from which he will soon be free. He may for a while be held back from that which is evil, and yet he may be radically bad; or he may be constrained by force of temptation to that which is wrong, and yet his real self may rejoice in righteousness. A man may not certainly be pronounced to be good because for the moment he is doing good, nor may he be condemned as evil because under certain constraints he may be committing sin. A man's longings are more inward and more near to his real self than his outward acts; they are more natural in that they are entirely free and beyond compulsion or restraint. As a man longeth in his heart, so is he. I do not mean every idle wish, but I refer to the strong desires of the heart. These are the lifeblood of a man's nature. You can know whether you yourself are good or evil by answering the question, To which do you have the greatest desire? Do you continually long after selfish pleasures? Then you are evil, beyond all question. Do you sigh to be and do that which is good—is this the great aim of your life? Then in the core of your being there is some good thing toward the Lord God of Israel. Your heart-longings may furnish you with excellent helps for self-examination, and I beg you to apply them at once. The things of the heart touch the root of the matter. Unbelievers are "a people that do err in their heart" (Ps. 95:10), and men truly find the Lord when they "seek him with the whole heart" (Ps. 119:2). The heart is all-important, and its longings are among the surest marks of its condition.

Moreover, heart-longings are prophecies of what a person will be. It is not always capacity that signals what a man will do, for many individuals of enormous abilities achieve next to nothing for lack of motivation. Their talents lie hidden in the earth, and although they might have succeeded marvelously in certain pursuits, they do nothing at all remarkable because they have no tendencies in that direction. An individual may have the means to help the poor and yet never perform a charitable act from lack of liberality. He may have great mental powers and yet never produce a line of useful literature because he is eaten up with laziness. But other things being equal, the longings of a man are a pretty sure index of what the man will be. Longings cannot create capacity, but they develop it, they lead to the use of means for its increase, and they make the mind keen to seize on opportunities. By one way or another, a man usually becomes what he intensely longs to be, especially if those desires are formed in early youth. Hence our proverb: "The child is father to the man."

Even in little children, tastes and pursuits have been prophetic—the young artist sketches her sister in the cradle, the youthful engineer is busy with his inventions. If those longings deepen, strengthen, and intensify with the increase of years, the young person's character is surely being molded from within, and this is often a greater force than that of circumstances acting from without. Thus is it in spiritual things: we may form forecasts as to what we shall be from our burning and pressing desires. Desires are the buds out of which words and deeds will ultimately be developed. Spiritual desires are the shadows of coming blessings. What God intends to give us He first sets us to longing for. Hence the wonderful efficacy of prayer, because prayer is the embodiment of a longing inspired of God because He intends to bestow the blessing. What are your longings? Do you long to be holy? The Lord will make you holy. Do you long to conquer sin? You shall overcome it by faith in Jesus. Are you seeking fellowship with Christ? He will come and make His home with you. Does your soul thirst, yea, even pant after God as the hart for the water brooks (Ps. 42:1)? Then you shall be filled with all His fullness, for all these longings are prophetic of that which is to be, even as the snowdrop and crocus and anemone foretell the approach of spring. I did not say that it is so with all human wishes, but where there are intense, heartbreaking yearnings of a holy kind, you can depend upon it they are tokens of good things to come.

Where the grace of God reigns in the soul, it makes a man become a stranger to the world, and it cultivates in him distinct affections and new desires. The verse that precedes my text runs: "I am a stranger in the earth." David was a king surrounded by courtiers and friends, and yet he was not at home, but like one banished from his native land. And being thus a stranger in the earth, he had a remarkable desire that others could not understand, and that singular craving he here expresses: "My soul breaketh for the longing that it hath unto thy judgments at all times." Worldly men care nothing for the judgments of God; indeed, they care nothing for God Himself. But when a man becomes new born, a citizen of heaven, there grows up within his spirit a spiritual appetite of which he had felt nothing before, and he longs after God and His holy Word. See to it whether your souls cry out for God, for the living God, for again I say, by your longing you may test yourself, by your heart's desires you may forecast your future, and by your hungerings and thirstings you may judge whether you are of this world or a citizen of the world to come. With such aids to self-judgment, no one can remain in doubt as to his spiritual condition and eternal prospects.

The Saints' Absorbing Object

The saints long after God's judgments. The word *judgments* is here used as synonymous with the "Word of God." It does not mean those judgments of God with which He smites sinners and executes the sentence of His law, but it refers to the revealed will and declared judgments of God. All through this long psalm the writer is speaking of the Word of God, the law of God, the testimonies, the precepts, the statutes of God; and here the word *judgments* is used in the same sense. The commandments and doctrines of the Word are God's judgments about moral and spiritual things, His decisions as to what is right and wrong, and His solutions to the great problems of the universe. God's revealed plan of salvation is God's decision upon man's destiny, God's judgment of condemnation against human sin, and yet His judgment of justification on behalf of believing sinners, whom He regards as righteous through faith in Jesus Christ. The Bible may be rightly regarded as the book of divine judgments, the recorded sentences of the High Court of Heaven, the infallible decision of perfect holiness upon questions that concern our souls.

You may come to the Scriptures as men came to the throne of Solomon, where hard cases were at once met. Yet, a greater One than Solomon is here. Search God's Word and you will have before your eyes the ultimate judgment of unerring truth, the last decree from the supreme authority, from which there is no appeal. The Bible contains the verdicts of the Judge of all the earth, the judgments of God, who cannot lie and cannot err. Thus, God's Word is rightly called His "judgments." It is a book not to be judged by us but to be our judge: not a word of it may be altered or questioned, but to it we may constantly refer as to a court of appeal whose sentence is decisive.

David in our text tells us how he desired the Lord's judgments, or His Word. We understand from this that first, *he greatly reverenced the Word.* He was not among those who regard the Bible as a very important portion of human literature but as being no more inspired than the works of Shakespeare. As little as David had of the Scriptures, he had a solemn reverence for what he had and stood in awe of it. I have no objection to honest criticism of the keenest kind, but I am shocked at certain scholars who cut and carve the blessed Word as if it were some vile carcass given over to their butchery. Let us not forget whose book it is and whose words we are examining. There is a near approach to blasphemy against God Himself in irreverence to His Word. There is no book like this for authority and majesty. It is hedged about with solemn sanctions so that it has both a wall of fire round about it and a glory in its midst to make it distinct from all other writings. This book is solid gold, containing ingots, mines, even whole worlds of priceless treasure, nor could its contents be exchanged for pearls or rubies. Even in the mental wealth of the wisest men there are no jewels like the truths of God's revelation. The thoughts of men are vanity, the conceptions of men are low and grovelling at their best; and He who has given us this book has said, "My thoughts are not your thoughts. . . . For as the heavens are higher than the earth, so are . . . my thoughts than your thoughts" (Isa. 55:8–9). Let it be to you and to me a settled matter that the Word of the Lord shall be honored in our minds and enshrined in our hearts. Let others speak as they may: "My soul breaketh for the longing that it hath unto thy judgments." We could sooner part with all that is sublime and beautiful in human literature than lose a single syllable from the mouth of God.

But more: inasmuch as the Psalmist greatly reverenced God's Word, *he intensely desired to know its contents.* He probably had only the five books of Moses, but the Pentateuch was enough to fill his whole soul with delight. Never depreciate the Old Testament. Remember that the great things that are said in the Psalms about the Word of God were not spoken concerning the New Testament, although they may truly be applied to it. Yet they were originally spoken only concerning the first five books, so that the first part of the Bible, according to the Holy Spirit's own testimony, is to be valued beyond all price. Indeed, the substance of the New Testament is in those books. The lovely form of queenly truth is there, only her veil conceals her countenance. The clearer shining of the New Testament is not a different light, nor perhaps is it in itself brighter, but it shines through a thinner medium and therefore more fully enlightens us. The various books of Scripture do not increase in real value; they only advance in their adaption to us. The light is the same, but the lantern is clearer, and we see more.

The treasure of the gospel is contained in the mines of the books of Moses, and I do not wonder therefore that David, instinctively knowing it to be there but not being able to reach it, felt a great longing after it. He was not so well able to get at the truth as we are, since he did not have the life of Christ or the apostolic explanations to open up the truth. Therefore he sighed inwardly and felt a killing heartbreak of desire to reach that which he knew was laid up in store for him. If he had not been sure that the treasure was there, he would not have cried, "Open thou mine eyes, that I may behold wondrous things out of thy law" (Ps. 119:18). He was like a voyager on the verge of discovery who nevertheless cannot quite reach it. He was like a miner whose pick has struck upon a lump of metal, and he is sure that gold is there, but he cannot get it away from the quartz in which it is embedded. The more certain he is that it is there, and the harder it is to reach, the more insatiable does his desire become to possess the treasure. Hence, I see the reasonableness of the psalmist's vehement passion, and I marvel not that he cried, "My soul breaketh for the longing that it hath unto thy judgments at all times."

But I am sure that David did not merely want to know as a matter of intellectual pleasure, but *he wished to feed upon God's Word.* What a very different thing it is to feed upon the Word from the bare knowledge of it. You can teach a child many chapters out of the Bible, and yet the child may not have fed on a word of it. Undoubtedly many know the history, the doctrine, and the letter of God's Word as well as others know their Homer or their Virgil, and so far, so good. But oh, to feed upon the Word of God is quite another thing. An oven full of bread is good, but for nourishment, a loaf on the table is better, and a morsel in the mouth is better still. In like manner, truth in a sermon is to be valued, truth attentively heard comes nearer to practical benefit, truth believed is better still; and truth absorbed into the spiritual system is best of all.

Alas, I fear we are not so absorbent as we should be. I like to see people who can be spiritual sponges to God's truth—suck it right up and take it into themselves. It would be better, however, that they should not be so much like sponges as to part with the truth when the hands of the world attempt to wring it out of them. I say that we are not receptive enough, because our hearts are not in tune with God. Do we not feel at times that certain truths of the Word are hardly in our mind? Our judgment must be daily more and more conformed to the judgments of God that are laid down in Scripture, and there must be in our spirit a longing after holiness until we delight in the law of the Lord and meditate upon it both day and night. We shall grow to the likeness of that which we feed upon: heavenly food will make us heavenly minded. The Word received into the heart changes us into its own nature, and by rejoicing in the decisions of the Lord, we learn to judge after His judgment and to delight ourselves in that which pleases Him. This sense, I think, comes nearer to the explanation of David's intense longings.

Doubtless, David *longed to obey God's Word*—he wished in everything to do the will of God without fault either in omission or in commission. He prays in another place, "Teach me, O LORD, the way of thy statutes, and I shall keep it unto the end" (Ps. 119:33). Do you long after perfection in that same fashion? All who truly know God must have a mighty yearning to run in the way of the Lord's commandments. He does not live before God who does not crave to live like God. There is no regeneration where there are no aspirations after holiness. The actual practice of obedience is necessary as a proof of the possession of true grace, for the rule is invariable, "By their fruits ye shall know them" (Matt. 7:20). No man knows the Word of God till he obeys it: "If any man will do his will, he shall know the doctrine" (John 7:17).

The Psalmist also *longed to feel the power of God's judgments in his own heart*. You know something about this if the Spirit of God has had dealings with you. Have you not felt the Lord judging you in the chamber of your conscience? The Spirit comes by the Word and sets our iniquities before us, our secret sins in the light of His countenance. You had forgotten the wrong, or at least, you hardly remembered it as a sin, but suddenly you saw it all. As I have looked upon a landscape under a cloudy sky, a gleam of sunlight has suddenly fallen upon one portion of it and made it stand out brilliantly from the midst of the surrounding gloom. So has the Holy Spirit poured a clear light upon some act or set of acts of my life, and I have seen it as I never saw it before. That inner light has judged us and led us to seek fresh cleansing: the judgments of God have come into our souls and led us anew to cry for mercy. I have found it so, have not you?

The Lord will judge His people and make sin bitter to them. Should we wish for this? I say, *yes*. Every true man should feel a longing in his own soul to have every sin within him exposed, condemned, and executed. He should wish to hide nothing, but to be revealed unto himself and humbled by the sight. We must undergo either judgment in the forum of our conscience or judgment before the great white throne at last. You must either condemn yourself or be condemned. God justifies those who condemn themselves, and none but these shall ever obtain the righteousness that is of God by faith. Hence, we may cry to be emptied that grace may fill us. David desires that God's Word would come right into him and hold its court of judgment. He came to feel this process to be so necessary that his soul broke with the longing that he had to be dealt with by God after this fashion. This is wisdom and prudence when a man so desires sanctification that he is distressed in his soul until the painful processes are being carried on by which his purity is to be produced. It is a wise child who will, for the sake of health, desire to take the prescribed medicine. God's children are not far from being well when they have reached such a point of sacred judgment.

This is the wish of all true believers—*to be perfectly conformed to the judgments of God.* Some of us can honestly say that we would not have a second wish for ourselves if our heavenly Father would grant us this one—that we might be perfect even as He is. We would leave all other matters with Him as to wealth or poverty, health or sickness, honor or shame, life or death, if He would but give us complete conformity to His own will. This is the object of the craving, yearning, and sighing of our souls. We hunger to be holy. Here I must correct myself as to our one desire, for surely if the Lord would make us holy, we should then desire that all other people would be the same. Oh, that the world were converted to God! Oh, that the truth of God would go forth like the brightness of the morning! Would God that every error and superstition might be chased away like bats and owls before the rising of the sun! O God, Your servants long for this. We ask for nothing save these two things: first, reign, O Lord, in the triple kingdom of our nature, and then reign over all nature. Let the whole earth be filled with Your glory, and our prayers are ended.

The Saints' Ardent Longings

First, let me say of these longings that *they constitute a living experience,* for dead things have no aspirations or cravings. You can visit the graveyard and exhume all the bodies you please, but you shall find neither desire nor craving. Longings do not linger within a lifeless corpse. Where the heart is breaking with desire, there is life. This may comfort some of you: you have not attained as yet to the holiness you admire, but you long for it. Ah, then, you are a living soul, the life of God is in you. You have not yet come to be conformed to the precept, but oh how you wish you were! That wish proves that a spark of the divine life is in your soul. The stronger that longing becomes, the stronger is the life from which it springs. Can you say that your heart longs for God as the watcher through the midnight sighs for the dawn or as the traveler over burning sand longs for the shadow of a great rock? Though I would not have you rest in longings, yet they are a proof that you are spiritually alive. Heart-longings are far better tests than attendance at meetings. Eager desires prove spiritual life much better than supposed attainments, for these supposed attainments may all be imaginary, but a heart breaking for the longing that it has to God's Word is no fancy; it is a fact too painful to be denied.

Next, recollect the expression used in our text *represents a humble sense of imperfection.* David had not yet come to be completely conformed to God's judgments or to know them perfectly, or else he would not have said that he longed for them. So it is with us. We have not reached perfection, but let us not therefore be discouraged, for the apostle to the Gentiles said, "Not as though I had already attained, either were already perfect" (Phil. 3:12). The man after God's own heart, even David, when he was at his best says not so much that he had obtained anything as that he longed after it, not so much that he had yet grasped it but sought for it: "My soul breaketh for the longing that it hath." All good men long to be better, and better men desire to be best of all, that they may dwell in heaven. The more grace the saints have, the more they desire: sacred greed is begotten by the possession of the love of God.

Furthermore, the expression of the text *indicates an advanced experience.* Saint Augustine dwells upon this idea, for he rightly says that at first there is an aversion in the heart to God's Word, and to desire after it is a matter of growth. After the aversion is removed, there often comes an indifference in the heart. It is no longer opposed to godliness, but it does not care to possess it. Then, through divine grace, there springs up in the soul a sense of the beauty of God's Word and will and an admiration of holiness. This leads on to a measure of desire after the good thing and a degree of appetite for it. But it shows a considerable growth in grace when we ardently long after it and a still larger growth when the soul breaks because of these longings. The text represents the agonizing of an earnest soul. Such a state shows a considerable advancement in the divine life, but when a believer has those desires "at all times," he is not far from being a mature Christian. "Oh," say you, "he thinks so little of what he has that he is crushed under the burden of desire for more." Yes, and he is the very man who has the most spiritual wealth. Those desires are mysterious entries in the account book of his heart, and rightly read they prove his wealth, for in the divine life, the more a man desires, the more he has already obtained. You may make tallies of your desires, and as you reckon by those tallies, they shall tell you to a penny what your spiritual wealth is. The more full a man is of grace, the more he hungers for grace.

It is an experience that I cannot quite describe to you, except by saying that it is *a bitter sweet*, or rather, a sweet bitter, if the adjective is to be stronger than the noun. There is a bitterness about being crushed with desire; it is inevitable that there should be, but the aroma of this bitter herb is inexpressibly sweet. No perfume can excel it. After all, a bruised heart knows more peace and rest than a heart filled with the world's delights. How safe such a soul is. Better to feel a heavenly hunger than a worldly fullness. Heartbreak for God is a sweeter thing than content in sinful pleasures. There is an inexpressible sweetness, a dawning of heaven, in longing after God; and yet, because you feel you have not yet attained what you desire, there is a bitter mixed with it. Pangs of strong desire increase our overflowing pleasures, and longings and hungerings make attainings and enjoyings to be all the more delightful. May the Lord send us more of this lamb with bitter herbs, this mingled experience in which we are "sorrowful, yet always rejoicing" (2 Cor. 6:10).

Still, those longings after God's Word may *become very wearing to a man's soul*. The sense of our text in the Hebrew is that of attrition or wearing down. The longings wear out the man when they become so fervent as those confessed in the text. I believe that some of the Lord's holy ones have been worn down to sickness and depression by the passion of their hearts after God. Their souls have become like sharp swords that cut through their scabbards, for they have destroyed the body by intense inner desires. At times holy men draw so near to God and long so greatly after His glory that for half a word they would pass the frontier and enter into heaven. They are so fully in accord with God that the shell that shuts in their soul is almost broken, and the newborn spirit is ready for its fullest life and liberty. How blessed to shake off the last fragment of that which holds us back from the freedom of an immortal life in perfect agreement with God. Oh, to attain to this! One saint cried, "Let me see the face of God," and another answered, "You cannot see God's face and live," to which he replied, "Then let me see my God and die."

Are you searching yourself to see whether you have such longings? If so, do you have them "at all times"? We are not to long for God's Word and will by fits and starts. We are not to have desires awakened by novelty or by excitement, nor are we to long for divine things, because for a while temporal things fail us—we are sick and sorry and weary of the world, and so in disgust we turn to God. I trust you long after God when all is bright in providence and that you love His Word when all is pleasant in family affairs. It is good to desire the Lord's will when He is permitting you to have your own will as well as when He is thwarting you. God is to be always our delight. He is our defense in war, but He is also our joy in peace. Do not use Him as sailors use those harbors of refuge for which they are not bound, into which they run only in time of storm. The Lord's will is to be the path of our feet and Himself the element of our life. This is to be a true child of God, *always* to have a yearning soul toward God's commandments. May the Holy Spirit keep us ever hungering and thirsting after God and His truth.

Words of Comfort

Perhaps you have been saying, "There are comforting thoughts for me in all this. I have not grown much, I have not done much, I wish I had; but I have strong longings, I am very dissatisfied, and I am almost ready to die with desire after Christ." My dear soul, listen—let this encourage you. First, *God is at work in your soul.* Never did a longing after God's judgments grow up in the soul of itself. Weeds come up by themselves, but the rarer kind of plants will never be found where there has been no sowing. And this flower, this plant of intense eagerness after God, never sprang up in the human heart by itself. God alone has placed it there. Friend, there was a time when you had no such longing. And if left to yourself, you would never have such a longing again. Come, then, God is at work in your soul—let this comfort you. The great Potter has you yet upon the wheel and has not cast you away as worthless. His work may pain you, but it is honorable and glorious. Your heart may swell with unutterable longings, and it may be torn by throes of desire, but life thus proves its presence and reaches forth to something yet beyond. These pains of desire are the Lord's doings and should be perceived with gratitude.

The result of God's work is very precious. Though it may be only a gracious desire, thank God for it. Though you can get no further than holy longing, be grateful for that longing. I would have you strive for the highest gifts, but I would not have you despise what God has already given you. Perhaps you have been racked with sighs, groans, cravings, and other forms of unrest and you have said, "O God, deliver me from this sore travail"; but when within a week you have had to lament lukewarmness, you have cried, "Lord, put me back again into my state of desire! Lord, set me hungering and thirsting again; a fierce appetite is better than this deadness." Be thankful, you that are longing, that you do long, for you have a rich promise to cheer you, since it is written, "He will fulfill the desire of them that fear him" (Ps. 145:19). The more wretched and unhappy you are under a sense of sin, the more grateful you should be for tenderness of heart. And the more you are longing to lay hold on Christ and to become like Christ, the more you should thank God that He has wrought this selfsame thing in you. How sweet is that word: "LORD, thou has heard the desire of the humble: thou wilt prepare their heart, thou wilt cause thine ear to hear" (Ps. 10:17).

Hearken once again: not only is the desire precious, but *it is leading on to something more precious.* Hear that which is written: "The desire of the righteous shall be granted" (Prov. 10:24). What do you say to such words as these? "When the poor and needy seek water, and there is none, and their tongue faileth for thirst, I the LORD will hear them, I the God of Israel will not forsake them" (Isa. 41:17). Do you think that God prompts us to desire a thing that He does not mean to give us? Is that the way you treat your children? You would not hold a sweet before a poor child, promise it to him, and then refuse him to taste it: that were a cruel pastime. God is not unkind. If He makes you hungry, for that hunger He has made ready the bread of heaven. If He makes you thirst, for that thirst He has already filled the river of the water of life. If the desire comes from God, the supply of that desire will as certainly come from God. Rest assured of that and cry mightily to Him with strong faith in His goodness.

Meanwhile, *the desire itself is doing you good*. It is driving you out of yourself, making you feel what a poor creature you are in your own nature. It is compelling you to look to God alone. Come readily to your Lord. Be one of those vessels that can sail with a capful of wind. Come by faith to Jesus, even though you fear that your desires are by no means so vivid and intense as those of my text. Believe, and you shall be established. Rest assured that there is in God whatever your soul wants. In Christ Jesus dwells all the fullness of the Godhead bodily, and in that divine fullness there must of necessity be more than a creature can require. In Christ Jesus there is exactly what your soul is panting for.

This is the blessedness of this longing after God's judgments, that *it makes Christ precious*. We see all God's Word in Christ; we see all God's decisions against sin and for righteousness embodied in our Savior; we see that if we can get Christ, we have then found the wisdom and power of God and, in fact, the all-sufficiency of God. If we can become like Christ, we shall be like God Himself. This, I say, makes Christ so precious and makes us long to get more fully to know Him and to call Him ours. Come to my Lord Jesus even now! Come, you who are bursting with wishes and desires, come and trust the Savior. Rest in Him now. May this be the moment in which you shall find how true it is: "Blessed are they which do hunger and thirst after righteousness: for they shall be filled" (Matt. 5:6). May you yet sing the Virgin's song, "My soul doth magnify the Lord . . . He hath filled the hungry with good things" (Luke 1:46, 53).

*S*eeing God means much more than perceiving traces of Him in nature, in the Scriptures, and in His church. Seeing God means that the pure in heart begin to discern something of God's true character. Anyone who is caught in a thunderstorm and hears the crash of the thunder and sees what havoc the lightning flashes work, perceives that God is mighty. But to perceive that God is eternally just and yet infinitely tender and that He is sternly severe and yet immeasurably gracious and to see the various attributes of the Deity all blending into one another as the colors of the rainbow make one harmonious and beautiful whole—this is reserved for the person whose eyes have been first washed in the blood of Jesus and then anointed with heavenly eye salve by the Holy Spirit. It is only such a person who sees that God is always and altogether good and who admires Him under every aspect, seeing that all His attributes are beautifully blended and balanced and that each attribute sheds additional splendor upon all the rest. The pure in heart shall in that sense see God, for they shall appreciate His attributes and understand His character as the ungodly never can.

Chapter Ten

The Sixth Beatitude

Blessed are the pure in heart: for they shall see God—Matthew 5:8.

IT WAS A DISTINGUISHING CHARACTERISTIC of the great Apostle and High Priest of our profession, Jesus Christ our Lord and Savior, that His teaching was continually aimed at the hearts of men. Other teachers had been content with outward moral reformation, but He sought the source of all the evil, that He might cleanse the spring from which all sinful thoughts and words and actions come. He insisted over and over again that until the heart was pure, the life would never be clean. The memorable Sermon on the Mount, from which our text is taken, begins with the benediction, "Blessed are the poor in spirit," for Christ was dealing with men's spirits—with their inner and spiritual nature. He did this more or less in all the Beatitudes, and this one strikes the very center of the target as He says, not "Blessed are the pure in language or in action," much less "Blessed are the pure in ceremonies or in clothing or in food," but "Blessed are the pure *in heart.*"

While a so-called religion may recognize as its follower a person whose heart is impure, the religion of Jesus Christ will not. Christ's message to all people still is "Ye must be born again" (John 3:7); that is, the inner nature must be divinely renewed or you cannot enter or even see the kingdom of God that Jesus came to set up in this world. If your actions appear to be pure, yet if the motive at the back of those actions is impure, that will nullify them all. If your language is virtuous, yet if your heart is revelling in foul imaginations, you stand before God not according to your words but according to your desires. By virtue of the current of your affections—your real inward likes and dislikes—you shall be judged by Him. External purity is all that man asks at our hands, "for man looketh on the outward appearance, but the LORD looketh on the heart" (1 Samuel 16:7); and the promises and blessings of the covenant of grace belong to those who are made pure in heart, and to no one else.

In focusing our attention upon the text, I want to first show you that *impurity of heart is the cause of spiritual blindness.* I will next show that *the purification of the heart admits us to a most glorious sight:* "the pure in heart shall see God." Then I shall have to show you that *the purification of the heart is a divine operation* that cannot be performed by ourselves or by any human agency. Holiness must be wrought in our lives by Him who is the thrice-holy Lord God.

Impurity of Heart Is the Cause of Spiritual Blindness

A drunk man cannot see clearly; his vision is often distorted or doubled. There are other cups besides alcohol that prevent the mental eye from having clear sight. He who has once drunk deeply of those cups will become spiritually blind, and others, in proportion as they imbibe the poisonous drinks, will be unable to see ahead.

There are moral beauties and immoral horrors that certain people cannot see because they are impure in heart. Take, for instance, the covetous person, and you will soon see that there is no other dust that blinds so completely as gold dust. There are many trades that are regarded as bad from top to bottom; but if the trade pays the man who is engaged in it, and he is greedy, it will be almost impossible to convince him that it is an evil trade. You will usually find that the covetous person sees no charm in generosity. He thinks that the giving person, if not actually a fool, is so near akin to one that he might very easily be mistaken for one. He himself admires what can be most easily grasped, and the more of it that he can secure, the better is he pleased. Making a fast deal and taking advantage of the poor are occupations in which he takes delight. If he has performed a dirty trick in which he has sacrificed every principle of honor, yet if it has turned out to his own advantage, he says to himself, "That was a clever stroke." If he meets another man of his own kind, he and his fellow will chuckle over the transaction and say how beautifully they had pulled it off. It would be useless for me to attempt to reason with a greedy man, to show him the beauty of giving. On the other hand, I would be wasting my time to try to get from him a fair opinion as to the justice of anything that he knew to be remunerative. You will recall that the Civil War was fought over the question of slavery. Who were the gentlemen in England who took the side of the slaveowners? Why, mostly Liverpool men, who did so because slavery paid them. If it had not paid them, they would have condemned it. And I daresay that those of us who condemned it did so the more quickly because it did not pay us. Men can see very clearly where there is nothing to be lost either way, but if it comes to be a matter of personal gain, the heart being impure, the eyes cannot see straight. There are innumerable things that a man cannot see if he holds a gold coin over each of his eyes—not even the sun. And if he keeps the coins over his eyes long enough, he will become blind. The pure in heart can see, but when covetousness gets into the heart, it makes the eye dim or blind.

Take another sin—the sin of oppression. There are people who actually tell us that in their opinion the persons who are in the highest positions in life are the very beauty and glory of the nation. They also say that poor people should be kept in their proper places because they were created for the purpose of "the nobility's" being sustained in their exalted position and that other highly respectable persons might gather to themselves any quantity of wealth. As to the idea of men wanting more money for their services, it must not be encouraged for a single moment, so these gentlemen say. If the poor seamstress toils and starves on the little money she can earn, you must not say a word about it. There are "the laws of political economy" that govern all such cases, so she must be ground between the wheels that abound in this age of machinery, and nobody should interfere! Of course, an oppressor cannot and will not see the evil of oppression. If you put before him a case of injustice that is as plain as the nose on his face, he cannot see it, because he has always been under the delusion that he was sent into the world with a whip in his hand to drive other people about. He feels he is the one great somebody and other people are nobodies, fit only to creep under his towering body and humbly ask his permission to live. In this way, oppression, if it gets into the heart, completely blinds the eye and perverts the judgment of the oppressor.

The same remark is true concerning lasciviousness. I have often noticed that when men have railed at religion and reviled the holy Word of God, their lives have been impure. Seldom, if ever, have I met a case in which my judgment has deceived me with regard to the lives of men who have spoken against holy things. I remember preaching once in a country town just about harvest time, and in commenting on the fact that some farmers would not let the poor have any gleanings from their fields, I said I thought there were some who were so mean that if they could rake their fields with a small-tooth comb they would do so. Thereupon, a farmer marched angrily out of the place. When he was asked why he was so wrathful, he answered, "Because I always rake my fields twice." Of course, he could not perceive any particular pleasure in caring for the poor; neither could he submit with a good grace to the rebuke that came home to him so pointedly. And when men speak against the gospel, it is almost always because the gospel speaks against them. The gospel has found them out; it has charged them with the guilt of their sins and has arrested them. It has come to them like a policeman and fully exposed their iniquity, and therefore they are indignant. They would not be living as they are if they could see themselves as God sees them. They would not be able to continue in their filthiness, corrupting others as well as ruining themselves, if they could really see. But as these evil things get into the heart, they are certain to blind the eyes.

The same thing may be said with regard to spiritual truth as well as moral truth. We frequently meet with people who say that they cannot understand the gospel of Christ. At the bottom, in nine cases out of ten, I believe that it is their sin that prevents their understanding it. For instance, I preached about the claims of God upon our lives. There may have been some of my hearers who said, "We do not recognize the claims of God to us." If any one talks like that, it is because their heart is not right in the sight of God. If they were able to judge righteously, they would see that the highest claims in all the world are those of the Creator upon His creatures, and they would immediately say, "I recognize that He who has created has the right to govern—that He should be Master and Lord who is both greatest and best—and that He should be Lawgiver who is infallibly wise and just and always kind and good." When men practically say, "We would not cheat or rob our fellowmen, but as for God, what does it matter how we treat Him?," the reason is that they are unjust in heart and their so-called justice to their fellowmen is only because their motto is "Honesty is *the best policy.*" They are not really just in heart, or they would at once admit the just claims of the Most High.

The great central doctrine of the atonement can never be fully appreciated until a man's heart is rectified. You have probably often heard such remarks as these: "I don't see why there should be any payment made to God for sin. Why could He not forgive transgression at once and be done with it? What need is there for a substitutionary sacrifice?" Ah, sir! If you had ever felt the weight of sin upon your conscience, if you had ever learned to loathe the very thought of evil, if you had been brokenhearted because you have been so terribly defiled by sin, you would feel that the atonement was required not only by God but also by your own sense of justice. Instead of rebelling against the doctrine of a vicarious sacrifice, you would open your heart to it and cry, "That is precisely what I need." The purest-hearted people who have ever lived are those who have rejoiced to see God's righteous law vindicated and magnified by Christ's death upon the cross as the Substitute for all who believe in Him, so that while God's mercy is displayed in matchless majesty, intensest satisfaction is felt that there could be a way of reconciliation by which every attribute of God should derive honor and glory and yet poor lost sinners should be lifted up into the high and honorable position of children of God. The pure in heart see no difficulty in the atonement; all the difficulties concerning it arise from the lack of purity there.

The same may be said of the equally important truth of regeneration. The impure in heart cannot see any need of being born again. They say, "We admit that we are not quite all that we should be, but we can easily take care of that. As to the talk about a new creation, we do not see any need of that. We have made some mistakes that will be rectified by experience, and there have been some errors of life that we trust may be condoned by future watchfulness and care." But if the unrenewed man's heart were pure, such a man would see that his nature had been an evil thing from the beginning. He would realize that thoughts of evil as naturally rise in us as sparks do from a fire, and he would feel that it would be a dreadful thing that such a nature as that should remain unchanged. He would see within his heart jealousies, murders, rebellions, and evils of every kind, and his heart would cry out to be delivered from itself. But because his heart is impure, he does not see his own impurity and does not and will not confess his need to be made a new creature in Christ Jesus. But as for you who are pure in heart, what do you now think of your old nature? Is it not the heavy burden that you continually carry about with you? Is not the plague of your own heart the worst plague under heaven? Do you not feel that the very tendency to sin is a constant grief to you and that if you could but get rid of it altogether, your heaven would have begun below? So it is the pure in heart who see the doctrine of regeneration, and those who see it not, see it not because they are impure in heart.

A similar remark is true concerning the glorious character of our blessed Lord and Master, Jesus Christ. Who has ever found fault with His character except men with bats' eyes? There have been unconverted men who have been struck with the beauty and purity of Christ's life, but the pure in heart are enamored of it. They feel that it is more than a human life—that it is divine, and that God Himself is revealed in the person of Jesus Christ His Son. If any man does not see the Lord Jesus Christ to be thus superlatively lovely, it is because he is himself not purified in heart. If he were pure in heart, he would recognize in Him the mirror of all perfection and would rejoice to do reverence to Him. But alas! It is still true that as it is with moral matters, so is it with that which is spiritual, and therefore the great truths of the gospel cannot be perceived by those whose heart is impure.

There is one form of impurity that beyond all others seems to blind the eye to spiritual truth, and that is duplicity of heart. A man who is single-minded, honest, sincere, childlike, is the man who enters the kingdom of heaven when its door is opened to him. The things of the kingdom are hidden from the double-minded and the deceitful, but they are plainly revealed to the babes in grace—the simplehearted, transparent people who wear their heart upon their sleeve. It is quite certain that the hypocrite will never see God while he continues in his hypocrisy. In fact, he is so blind that he cannot see anything, and certainly cannot see himself as he really is in God's sight. The man who is quite satisfied with the name of a Christian without the life of a Christian will never see God nor anything at all until his eyes are divinely opened. What does it matter to anybody else what his opinion is upon any subject whatever? We should not care to have praise from the man who is double-minded and who is practically a liar, for while he is one thing in his heart, he endeavors to pass himself off for another thing in his life.

Formalism, too, will never see God, for formalism always looks to the shell and never gets to the kernel. Formalism licks the bone but never gets to the marrow. It heaps to itself ceremonies, mostly of its own invention; and when it has attended to these, it flatters itself that all is well, though the heart itself still lusts after sin. The widow's house is being devoured even at the very time when the Pharisee is making long prayers in the synagogue or at the corners of the streets (Matt. 23:14). Such a person cannot see God. There is a kind of reading of the Scriptures that will never lead a man to see God. He opens the Bible, not to see what is there but to see what he can find to back up his own views and opinions. If the texts he wants are not there, he will twist others round till he somehow or other gets them on his side. But he will believe only as much as agrees with his own preconceived notions. He would like to mold the Bible, like a cake of wax, to any shape he pleases; so, of course, he cannot see the truth, and he does not want to see it.

The crafty men, too, never see God. I am afraid for no man more than the crafty, the man whose guiding star is "policy." I have seen rough sailors converted to God and blasphemers, harlots, and great sinners of almost all kinds brought to the Savior and saved by His grace. Very often they have told the honest truth about their sins, blurting out the sad truth in a very outspoken fashion. When they have been converted, I have often thought that they were like the good ground of which our Savior spoke (Matt. 13:23), with an honest and good heart in spite of all their badness. But as for the men of snakelike nature who say to you when you talk to them about religion, "Yes, yes," but do not mean it at all—the men who are never to be trusted: Mr. Smoothtongue, Mr. Facingbothways, Mr. Fairspeech, and all that class of people—God Himself never seems to do anything but let them alone. So far as my observation goes, God's grace seldom seems to come to these double-minded men who are unstable in all their ways. These are the people who never see God.

It has been remarked that our Lord probably alluded to this fact in the verse that forms our text. In Oriental countries, the king seldom was seen. He lived in retirement, and to get an interview with him was a matter of great difficulty. There were all sorts of plots and plans and intrigues and perhaps the use of backstairs influence that a man may at last get to see the king. But Jesus Christ says, in effect, "That is not the way to see God." No. No one ever gets to Him by craftiness—plotting and planning and scheming— but the simpleminded man who goes humbly to Him, just as he is, and says, "My God, I desire to see You; I am guilty, and I confess my sin and plead with You, for Your dear Son's sake, to forgive it," he it is who sees God.

I also think there are some Christians who never see God as well as other believers. Some brethren seem naturally of a questioning spirit. They are usually puzzled about some doctrinal point or other, and their time is mostly taken up with answering objections and removing doubts. Meanwhile, some poor humble countrywoman, who sits in the aisle and who knows nothing more than that her Bible is true and that God always keeps His promises, sees a great deal more of God than the learned and quibbling brother who troubles himself about foolish questions that benefit no one.

I know a minister who, calling on a sick woman, desired to leave a text with her for her private meditation. So, opening her old Bible, he turned to a certain passage, which he found that she had marked with the letter P. "What does that P mean?" he asked. "That means *precious*, sir. I found that text very precious to my soul on more than one special occasion." He looked for another promise, and against this he found in the margin T and P. "And what do these letters mean?" "They mean *tried and proved*, sir, for I tried that promise in my greatest distress and proved it to be true, and then I put that mark against it so that the next time I was in trouble, I might be sure that promise was still true." The Bible is scored all over with those *T*s and *P*s by generation after generation of believers who have tested the promises of God and proven them to be true. May you and I be among those who have thus tried and proven this precious Book!

The Purification of the Heart Admits Us to a Most Glorious Sight

"The pure in heart *shall see God.*" What does that mean? First, it means that *the man whose heart is pure will be able to see God in nature.* When his heart is clean, he will hear God's footfall everywhere in the garden of the earth in the cool of the day. He will hear God's voice in the tempest, sounding in peal on peal from the tops of the mountains. He will behold the Lord walking on the great and mighty waters or see Him in every leaf that trembles in the breeze. Once the heart is made right, God can be seen everywhere. To an impure heart, God cannot be seen anywhere, but to a pure heart, God is to be seen everywhere—in the deepest caverns of the sea, in the lonely desert, in every star that gems the brow of midnight.

Further, *the pure in heart see God in the Scriptures.* Impure minds cannot see any trace of God in them, but they see reasons for doubting whether Paul wrote the Epistle of Hebrews. They find reasons to doubt the canonicity of the Gospel of John, and that is about all that they see in the Bible. But the pure in heart see God on every page of this blessed Book. As they read it devoutly and prayerfully, they bless the Lord that He has been pleased to so graciously reveal Himself to them by His Spirit. They gratefully realize that He has given them the opportunity and the desire to enjoy the revelation of His holy will.

Besides that, *the pure in heart see God in His church.* The impure in heart cannot see Him there at all. To them, the church of God is nothing but a conglomeration of divided sects, and looking upon these sects, they can see nothing but faults, failures, and imperfections. It should always be remembered that every man sees that which is according to his own nature. When the vulture soars in the sky, he sees the carrion wherever it may be, and when the dove on silver wings mounts up to the azure, she sees the clean winnowed corn wherever it may be. The lion sees his prey in the forest, and the lamb see its food in the grassy meadow. Unclean hearts see little or nothing of good among God's people, but the pure in heart see God in His church and rejoice to meet Him there.

But seeing God means much more than perceiving traces of Him in nature, in the Scriptures, and in His church. Seeing God means that *the pure in heart begin to discern something of God's true character.* Anyone who is caught in a thunderstorm and hears the crash of the thunder and sees what havoc the lightning flashes work, perceives that God is mighty. But to perceive that God is eternally just and yet infinitely tender and that He is sternly severe and yet immeasurably gracious and to see the various attributes of the Deity all blending into one another as the colors of the rainbow make one harmonious and beautiful whole—this is reserved for the person whose eyes have been first washed in the blood of Jesus and then anointed with heavenly eye salve by the Holy Spirit. It is only such a person who sees that God is always and altogether good and who admires Him under every aspect, seeing that all His attributes are beautifully blended and balanced and that each attribute sheds additional splendor upon all the rest. The pure in heart shall in that sense see God, for they shall appreciate His attributes and understand His character as the ungodly never can.

But more than that, *they shall be admitted into His fellowship.* When you hear some people talk about there being no God and no spiritual things, you need not be at all concerned at what they say, for they are not in a position that qualifies them to speak about the matter. For instance, an ungodly man says, "I do not believe there is a God, for I never saw Him." I do not doubt the truth of what he says, but when I tell him that I *have* seen Him, he has no more right to doubt my word than I have to doubt his. One day at a hotel restaurant, I was talking with a fellow minister about certain spiritual things when a gentleman who sat opposite us made this remark: "I have been in this world for sixty years, and I have never yet been conscious of anything spiritual." We thought it was very likely that what he said was perfectly true, and there are a great many more people in the world who might say the same as he did. But that only proved that *he* was not conscious of anything spiritual, not that others were not conscious of it. There are many other people who can say, "We are conscious of spiritual things. We have been—by God's presence among us—moved, and bowed, and carried forward, and cast down, and then lifted up into joy, and happiness, and peace. Our experiences are as true phenomena, at least to us, as any phenomena under heaven. We are not to be beaten out of our beliefs, for they are supported by innumerable undoubted experiences." "He that dwelleth in the secret place of the most High shall abide under the shadow of the Almighty" (Ps. 91:1). "But there is no such secret place," says one. How does he know that? If someone else comes and says, "Ah! But I am dwelling in that secret place under that shadow," what will the doubter say to him? He may call the believer a fool, but that does not prove that he is a fool. However, it may prove that the doubter is one, for the believer is as honest a man as the doubter and as worthy to be believed.

Some years ago a lawyer from America attended a religious meeting where he heard about a dozen people relating their Christian experience. He sat with his pencil in his hand and jotted down their evidence as they gave it. At last, he said to himself, "If I had a case in court, I would like to have these persons as witnesses, for I should feel that if I had their evidence on my side, I should win the case." Then he thought, "Well, I have ridiculed these people as fanatics, yet I would like their evidence in court upon other matters. They have nothing to gain by what they have been saying, so I should believe that what they have said is true." The lawyer was simple enough, or rather, wise enough and pure enough in heart to look at the matter correctly, and so he also came to see the truth—and to see God. Many of us could testify that there is such a thing as fellowship with God even here on earth, but men can enjoy it only in proportion as they give up their love of sin. They cannot talk with God after they have been talking filthiness. They cannot speak with God as a man speaks with his friend if they delight to mingle with the ungodly. The pure in heart may see God, and do see Him—not with the natural eye, but with their inner spiritual eye they see the great God who is a Spirit, and they have spiritual but very real communion with the Most High.

The expression, "They shall see God," may mean something else. As I have already said, those who saw Oriental monarchs were generally considered to be highly privileged persons. There were certain ministers of state who had the right to go in and see the king whenever they chose to do so, and the pure in heart have just such a right given to them to go in and see their King at all times. In Christ Jesus, they have boldness and access with confidence in coming to the throne of heavenly grace. Being cleansed by the precious blood of Jesus, they have become the ministers, that is, the servants of God, and He employs them as His ambassadors, sending them on high and honorable errands for Him. They may see Him whenever their business for Him entitles them to an audience with Him.

And, finally, *the time shall come when those who have thus seen God on earth shall see Him face to face in heaven.* Oh, the splendor of that vision! It is useless for me to attempt to write about it. We are one heartbeat away from knowing more about it than all the divines on earth could tell us. 'Tis but a thin veil that parts us from the glory-world. It may be torn in two at any moment, and then at once the pure in heart shall fully understand what it is to *see God.* May that be your portion forever and ever!

This Purification of the Heart Is a Divine Work

Believe me when I tell you that *it is never an unnecessary work.* No man (except the man Jesus Christ) was ever born with a pure heart. All have sinned. All need to be cleansed. There is none good; no, not one.

Let me also assure you that *this work was never performed by any ceremony.* Men may say what they please, but no application of water ever made a man's heart any better. Some tell us that in baptism—by which they mean baby sprinkling as a rule—they regenerate and make members of Christ—children of God and inheritors of the kingdom of heaven. But those who are sprinkled are no better than other people. They grow up in just the same way as others. The whole ceremony is useless, and worse than that, for it is contrary to the example and teaching of the Lord Jesus Christ. No aqueous applications, no outward ceremonies can ever affect the heart.

Neither can the heart be purified *by a process of outward refor-*

mation. The attempt has often been made to work from the outside to the inside, but it cannot be done. You might as well try to give a living heart to a marble statue by working upon the outside of it with a mallet and chisel. To make a sinner pure in heart is as great a miracle as if God were to make that marble statue live and breathe and walk.

The heart can be purified only by God's Holy Spirit. The Holy Spirit must come upon us and overshadow us, and when He thus comes to us, then is our heart changed, but never before that. When the Spirit of God comes to us, He cleanses the soul—to follow the line of our Savior's teaching in Matthew 5—by showing us our spiritual poverty: "Blessed are the poor in spirit." That is the first work of God's grace—to make us feel that we are poor, that we are nothing, that we are undeserving, ill-deserving, hell-deserving sinners. As the Spirit of God proceeds with His work, the next thing that He does is to make us mourn: "Blessed are they that mourn." We mourn to think that we should have sinned as we have done, we mourn after our God, we mourn after pardon; and then the great process that effectually cleanses the heart is the application of the water and the blood that flowed from the pierced side of Christ on the cross. Here it is that we find a double cure from the guilt and from the power of sin! When faith looks to the bleeding Savior, it sees in Him not merely pardon for the past but the putting away of the sinfulness of the present.

The angel said to Joseph, before Christ was born, "Thou shalt call his name JESUS: for he shall save his people from their sins" (Matt. 1:21). The whole process of salvation may be briefly explained in this manner. The Spirit of God finds us with foul hearts, and He comes and throws a divine light into us so that we see that they are foul. Then He shows that being sinners, we deserve to endure God's wrath, and we realize that we do. Then He says to us, "But that wrath was borne by Jesus Christ for you." He opens our eyes, and we see that Christ died for us—in our place. We look to Him, we believe that He died as our Substitute, and we trust ourselves with Him. Then we know that our sins are forgiven us for His name's sake, and the joy of pardoned sin goes through us with such a thrill as we never felt before; and the next moment the forgiven sinner cries, "Now that I am saved, now that I am pardoned, my Lord Jesus Christ, I will be Your servant forever. I will put to death the sins that put You to death; and if You will give me the strength to do so, I will serve You as long as I live!" The current of the man's soul ran before toward evil, but the moment that the man finds that Jesus Christ died for him and his sins are forgiven, the whole stream of his soul rushes in the other direction toward that which is right. And though he still has a struggle against his old nature, from that day forth the man is pure in heart—that is, his heart loves purity, his heart seeks after holiness, his heart longs for perfection.

Now he is the man who sees God, loves God, delights in God, longs to be like God, and eagerly anticipates the time when he shall be with God and see Him face to face. That is the process of purification that you may enjoy through the effectual working of the Holy Spirit! If you are willing to have it, it is freely given to you. If you truly desire the new heart and the right spirit, they will be graciously granted to you. There is no need for you to try to fit yourself to receive them. God is able to work them in you at this very moment. He who will wake the dead with one blast of the resurrection trumpet can change your nature with the mere volition of His gracious mind. He can create in you a new heart, renew a right spirit within you, and make you into a different person. The power of the Holy Spirit to renew the human heart is boundless. "Oh," says one. "I desire that He would renew my heart and change my nature!" If that is your heart's desire, send up that prayer to heaven now. Let not the wish die in your soul, but turn it into a prayer and then breathe it out to God, hearkening to what God has to say to you. It is this: "Come now, and let us reason together, saith the LORD: though your sins be as scarlet, they shall be as white as snow; though they be red like crimson, they shall be as wool" (Isa. 1:18); or this: "Believe on the Lord Jesus Christ, and thou shalt be saved" (Acts 16:31)—saved from your love of sin, saved from your old habits, and so completely saved that you shall become one of the pure in heart who see God.

But perhaps you ask, "What is it to believe in the Lord Jesus Christ?" It is to trust Him, to rely upon Him. You will never get rid of your troubles till you do, but you may be rid of them this very moment if you will but believe in Jesus. Though you have struggled in vain against your evil habits, though you have wrestled with them and resolved against them, only to be defeated by your giant sins and terrible passions, there is One who can conquer all your sins for you. There is One who is stronger than Hercules, who can strangle the hydra of your lust, kill the lion of your passions, and cleanse the Augean stable of your evil nature by turning the great rivers of blood and water of His atoning sacrifice right through your soul. He can make and keep you pure within.

Look to Him! He hung upon the cross, accursed of men, and God made Him to be sin for us, though He knew no sin, that we might be made the righteousness of God in Him. He was condemned to die as our Sin-offering that we might live forever in the love of God. Trust Him, trust Him! He has risen from the dead and gone up into His glory. He is at the right hand of God pleading for transgressors. Trust Him! You can never perish if you trust Him, but you shall live, with ten thousand times ten thousand more who have all been saved by grace, to sing of a mighty Savior, able to save to the uttermost all them who come to God by Him. God grant you may be among the pure in heart who shall see God, and never leave off seeing Him, and He shall have all the glory.

I will walk within my house with a perfect heart." The Christian at home should be scrupulous in every way within his house. We may have different rooms there, but in whatever room we are, we should seek to walk before God with a perfect heart. Alas, there are many professing believers who fail in this! I have reason to fear that some people who walk as saints abroad behave themselves like devils at home. It is a fact that a man is what he is at home. This is a simple but a crucial test of character. If a man does not make his family happy and if his example is not that of holiness in the domestic circle, he may make what pretension of godliness he likes, but his religion is worthless. The sooner he gets rid of such a profession, the better for himself, for then he may begin to know what he is and where he is and seek the Lord in spirit and truth. It is at home that the lack of true faith will do most damage. If you are a hypocrite and go into the world, the people who observe you will not be much influenced by your example. They will come to the conclusion that you are what you are, and they will treat you as such, and that will be the end of it. But that will not be so with your little son who sees his father's actions. He is not able to criticize, but he has a wonderful faculty for imitation. And mother, it is not likely that your daughter will begin to say, "Mother is inconsistent." No, she does not know that, but she will take it for granted that mother is right, and her character will be fashioned upon your pattern. As parents you can injure your children for life unless the grace of God prevents it.

Chapter Eleven

A Holy Resolve

I will behave myself wisely in a perfect way. O when wilt thou come unto me? I will walk within my house with a perfect heart—
Psalm 101:2.

THE HUNDREDTH PSALM is perhaps the best known song of praise in the Word of God. To sing "Make a joyful noise unto the Lord all ye lands" has been a habit of worshipers from generation to generation. It is somewhat significant that the hundred-and-first, which immediately follows it, should be such a practical psalm—all about how a man should walk in his house, how he should put away sin from his eyes and keep himself from evil companionship. It seems to teach us that the best praise is purity and that the best music in the world is holiness. If we would extol the Lord, the best way to do it is to labor to keep His mind before us and to walk in His commandments. The sweetest sounds that ever came from the organ pipes can never have so much melody in them as a life that is tuned to the example of Christ. If we obey, we praise. There is no praise that excels that which is like the praise of angels "that do his commandments, hearkening unto the voice of his word" (Ps. 103:20).

I suppose that this psalm was written by David about the time when he was invested with kingly authority and took the reins of government in his hands. Three times, you will remember, he was anointed king. First, in the house of his father, when "Samuel took the horn of oil, and anointed him in the midst of his brethren" (1 Sam. 16:13). The second time was at Hebron when "the men of Judah came, and there they anointed David king over the house of Judah" (2 Sam. 2:4). And a third time when all the elders of Israel came to the king seven and a half years later, "and king David made a league with them in Hebron before the LORD: and they anointed David king over Israel" (2 Sam. 5:3). With the solemn responsibilities of government in view, David sat down and considered how he would behave himself when he should come to the throne. This was the resolution that he passed and labored by the grace of God to carry out. It has been well said in this psalm, David was merry and wise. He was merry, for he said, "I will sing of mercy and judgment" (Ps. 101:1); and he repeated his resolution to sing by saying, "Unto thee, O LORD, will I sing." Such merriment as that is good for all of us to cultivate. We cannot sing too much when we sing to the Lord, and (provided that the songs are the songs of Zion) the more of them we sing and the merrier we are in singing them, the better. But David was also wise, for he sought to have spiritual holiness and passed this resolution: "I will behave myself wisely in a perfect way."

What a Comprehensive Resolution This Is!

"I will behave myself wisely in a perfect way." With a full knowledge of all the care it entailed on himself and with as clear an apprehension of all the risks of popularity it involved among his subjects, this was David's *deliberate choice*. Influenced by the grace of God he, like his son Solomon after him, chose wisdom as the principal thing and accounted the fear of the Lord as the choicest safeguard. Many a young man, if he were about to be promoted to a throne, would say, "I will behave myself grandly. I will make them know how sovereign is my word, how nobly I can play my part, how well a crown befits my head." David might have chosen an empty conceit, but he did better—he elected a discreet conduct. He said not "I will behave myself grandly" but "I will behave myself *wisely*." There are men, too, who, having David's opportunity, would have said, "I will have a merry time of it. Once let me mount to Israel's throne, I will give myself up to the full indulgence of every passion. There shall be nothing that my soul shall lust for but what my hand shall grasp. I will get myself all manner of the delights of the flesh with whatever enjoyments I can devise." Not so David. His deliberate choice was neither grandeur nor pleasure, but wisdom.

Perhaps this is the time for you to take stock of your moral resolutions. How are you acting? What have you chosen? You shall be happy indeed if the grace of God leads you to say, "I choose wisdom, the truest and best wisdom. Be it mine to live as God would have me live: understanding His testimonies and yielding obedience to His laws. I will behave myself wisely in a perfect way." I say it was David's deliberate choice. Oh, that every young man would follow his example! Oh, that each of us in our present condition and in full view of whatever prospects may be opening up before us might be led now, once for all, with the full consent of all our powers, to say, "Whatever happens to me, this is my resolution. I desire to behave wisely. Should others run after gain or fame, ease or luxury, let them. Let them make self their idol or follow after gold. As for me, my soul is made up to this one purpose. I would be wise, my God."

This choice of David was no doubt *suggested by a sense of necessity*. David felt that he needed to behave wisely. He was to be a king, and a foolish king is no ordinary fool. But alas for the misfortunes of a country whose king is a fool! You know what troubles came upon the Jewish nation through Rehoboam and others, who were too foolish to sway the scepter righteously. David could hardly fail to remember that as he succeeded the dynasty of Saul, Saul's descendants would survive and seek to regain the crown. Therefore, he would need to act very discreetly to preserve himself from the pretenders and their faction. He knew that enemies would be sure to track his course, that if they could find any fault with him they would. He needed, therefore, to have great wisdom. "Well," you say, "this lesson does not concern me, for I am not going to be king." Granted, that may be so, but you need wisdom in every level of society. The humblest maid, as a Christian, needs wisdom to do her duty and adorn her position. Those entrusted with children need peculiar wisdom, for a child's mind may be warped by a servant as well as by a superior teacher. If you are in business, you need wisdom in such an age as this, with competition so fierce and temptation so abundant. And I am sure, if you are a parent and you wish to see your children trained up in the fear of God, you have a task before you that might tax the wisdom of Solomon. Many parents have been injudicious with their children, to their own anguish of heart in later years. Your all is embarked in the momentous voyage of life. If you make shipwreck of the life that God has given you and the humble position in which he has placed you, it is your all, and to you it is as much a ruin as if you had been a monarch. You need to behave yourselves wisely whatever your vocation in the world may be.

Moreover, David recognized that *to behave wisely one must be holy*, for he says, "I will behave myself wisely in a *perfect* way." He felt he could not be wise if he were unacquainted with the true ideal of absolute unblemished perfection: wisdom lay there. Always remember this. In common life the wisest thing is the right, straight, undeviating course. The right thing is always the wisest. Sometimes it looks as if it really is necessary to go off the straight line and just take a shortcut. It *seems* so, but it *never is*. The tale of the shortcut is a book of lamentations from beginning to end. Thousands have tried it, but always with the same result. The wise man will keep along the king's highway, cost what it may. We have heard of young men who, under extraordinary pressure, have felt as if they must relax integrity a little to obey a boss and thus keep the position they hold. Well, from that time forward their nose has been to the grindstone as long as they have lived. If they had had the manliness, let alone the godliness, to do the right thing, it would have been the turning point in their entire career and would have saved them from a thousand sorrows.

But you do not need to be a philosopher to discover how you should act under any circumstances. The way to act in every case is to fear God and keep His commandments. Straight ahead! That is the way to go in every case. If the conscience of man is elastic, the law of the Lord is inflexible. "What, and lose all I have?" Yes. You will lose less by doing right than you can possibly lose by doing wrong, for if a man were to lose all the property he possessed by a right action, it were better than that he should lose his soul by deliberately choosing to avoid poverty or acquire wealth instead of seeking to abide in the favor of God. "I will behave myself wisely," said David. But he knew that the perfect way, the way of right, the way of God was the way of wisdom. You cannot find a wiser counsel than this: "to do justly, and to love mercy, and to walk humbly with thy God" (Mic. 6:8). Keep to the eternal principle that God has revealed. Keep to the sacred instinct that the Holy Spirit sows in every regenerate heart. Keep to the example of your Lord and Master, who has bought you with His precious blood. Should it cost you trouble, should it cost you your life, "it is better for thee to enter into life halt or maimed, rather than having two hands or two feet to be cast into everlasting fire" (Matt. 18:8). The perfect way is the wise way, and the wise way a perfect.

David seems to have felt that this resolution would cost him a great deal of effort and strength before he said with so much emphasis, "I *will* behave myself wisely in a perfect way." Though he does not say so much, he fully implies determination without power. My will or desire is to behave myself wisely; my dependence is on Him whose cause I espouse. The next clause—"O when wilt thou come unto me"—seems to say, "I must have more grace, and I must get it, too. I must have more help than I can ever find in myself. I must use every means of grace and call on God to be my helper in this matter, for whatever it may cost, I will behave myself wisely in a perfect way." David felt that his character was too important to be trifled with, that it must be of sterling metal or else it was mere dross, and that the actions of a person's life were too serious to be taken lightly.

It shocks me to my very soul when I hear some people talk about the doctrines of grace that are as dear to my heart as life itself. These people uphold the principles of grace while they ignore the practices of godliness, for their lives are inconsistent with their professions. I have known professing believers who never talk so well about theology as they do when they are half drunk and never seem to be so sound in the faith as when they can hardly stand on their legs. They will tell you that good works are nothing at all, and they glory in free grace. Ah, dear friend, God save you from being Mr. Talkative, who could lecture upon free grace but never felt the power of it. If the grace of God does not save a man from drunkenness, from lascivious conversation, from lies and lewdness, from slandering and scowling at your fellow Christians, then I think the grace of God must be a very different thing from what I read of in this precious Word of God. Either my judgment is at fault or your pretensions are spurious.

The grace of God comes freely as the sovereign distinguishing gift of heaven, but it comes into men's lives and makes them different in holiness of character. If a man shall say to me, "Character—I don't care anything about that," I am not quick to answer him. I think a friend was right when he said that he did not believe in a man's religion if his cat and his dog are not the better for it— if everybody in his house is not the better for it. If it does not make you, as a boss, gentler and kinder to your workers; if it does not make you, as a worker, more respectful and more diligent; if it does not make you, as a tradesman, more scrupulous and honest; if it does not make you, as a workman, less of an eye-servant; if it does not, in fact, make you more moral, if it does not make you more holy, you may well question whether you know anything of the grace of God in your soul at all. David did not say, "Well, God has washed me whiter than snow, and He has created a new heart and a right spirit within me. That is enough. As to my outward actions, what do they signify? We are not saved by works, you know: it is all of grace." Ah, but that is not the language of David or of any other legitimate child of God. It is this: "I will behave myself wisely in a perfect way." I have heard it said that where they talk a great deal about good works, you will not find them, but I hope among those of us who talk much about grace, good works will always be found. Where good works do not follow upon faith, such faith as there seems to be is dead, being alone.

The Need for Power

Many inspired writers, without diverging from their train of thought, interline their purpose with a prayer. There is an old proverb, "Kneeling never spoils silk stockings." Prayer to the preacher is like hay to the horse. It strengthens and cheers him to go forward. As the scribe halts to mend his pen or the mower to sharpen his blade without loss of time but rather with more facility to do this work, so you expedite instead of hinder your business by stopping in the middle of it to offer a word of prayer. So here it is written,

"O when wilt thou come unto me?," and David means by that, "Lord, I want to be wise. Come and teach me. I want to behave wisely. Lord, come and sanctify me. I know not how to act till You instruct me. Open my lips that I may show forth Your praise. Guide my feet that I may run in Your commands. Keep my eyes that they look not upon sin. Hold back my hand from iniquity. When will You come to me? I need the influence of Your grace to guide me in Your ways." Then he goes further, "Lord, come and assist me. If there is any holiness to which I have not yet attained, come, Holy Spirit, lift me up to it. If there is any sin that I have not conquered, come thou conquering Spirit of holiness and overcome the evil. When will You come to me? I can do nothing, but when I have Your mighty aid, I become strong and can perform all things." It is a crying of his soul after divine teaching, divine direction, divine assistance, and it is a yearning after divine fellowship.

We never walk uprightly unless we walk with God. As I have said that holiness is wisdom, so let me say that communion with God is the mother of holiness. We must see God if we are to be like God. If from day to day we can live contented without a word from the mouth of God—going to business without prayer, coming home and going to our beds without seeking the face of our Father who is in heaven—then, to walk wisely is impossible. The neglect of prayer is a fatal flaw in any life. Communion with God is so essential and the disregard of it is such a folly that it is simply ridiculous for the negligent man to talk about behaving himself in a perfect way. Godliness is the soul of life. Get near to God—that is the thing. If we walk with Him, we walk in the light, but if we get away from Him, we walk in the darkness. It cannot be otherwise, and he who walks in the darkness will stumble. He may not know on what he stumbles, but he will stumble. Only he who walks in the light will be able to pick his steps and verify the blessed fact: "But if we walk in the light, as he is in the light, we have fellowship one with another, and the blood of Jesus Christ his Son cleanseth us from all sin" (1 John 1:7). And thus we are enabled to walk wisely in a perfect way when the light comes to us.

"I will behave wisely . . . when wilt thou come unto me?" appears to me like an expression of holy awe, as if David had said, "Lord, I must obey for You are coming. I am a steward, You are my Master, and You are coming to say, 'Give an account of Your stewardship.' I need mind what I am about and how I acquit myself, for my Master can see me and is on the way to say to me, 'What have You done with Your talent?' When will You come to me? It makes me feel a trembling in my soul and brings tears into my eyes when I think of having to go before my Lord to give him my account. Such a stewardship as mine will not easily be accounted for." I often envy George Fox, the Quaker, who, as he died, used these remarkable words, "I am clear, I am clear, I am clear!" That is a grand thing for a minister to be able to say. It requires all the grace that God can give a man to be able to say that. Now I ask you, fathers of families, were you called upon at once without further notice to give an account, can you tell the Lord you are clear about your children? Mothers, can you say you are clear about your sons and daughters, as to the way you have brought them up—as to your efforts for their souls? In the workplace, are you clear about your employees? Young men, young women, are you clear about those that you work with and in whose house you live? If the Lord were to say to you, "Come, now, I have entrusted you with a talent, how have you used it?", are you prepared to answer? Am I ready? Am I able to give a satisfactory account as to what I have done as His servant in my general walk and conversation? God grant you to order your life by His grace. You cannot do so without the power of the Holy Spirit. Oh, that whenever the Lord shall come you may meet Him with joy.

Refocusing His Holy Resolve

"I will walk within my house with a perfect heart." With his house or household in view, for which he felt a deep responsibility and a yearning anxiety, David applies himself with a delicate consideration to the state of his own heart. "Keep thy heart with all diligence; for out of it are the issues of life" (Prov. 4:23). A very wise thing. Elisha healed the springs when the currents ran foul (2 Kings 2:19–22). It is of no use attempting to cleanse the courses when the fountain is corrupt. The thing is to heal the springs. The heart needs putting right. When the heart is right, all will be right. If anywhere we show our hearts, it is at home. There we wear our hearts upon our sleeves. Outside in the world it is not safe to show too much of our heart. There are some of us who always say everything we feel. We have not yet learned to be guarded, but we have had our knuckles rapped pretty dreadfully sometimes for it. No doubt there are many men of a reserved disposition who go through the world more easily than those of a more open-minded character. At home everybody should be openhearted and transparent. Hence the necessity that if we are to walk uprightly at home, the matter should begin with the heart being sound. The heart must be perfect, and then we must show our heart in our actions.

I think it is a miserable thing when a man does not open his heart in the sacred precincts of his own home. I can understand his restraining his feelings at work, for he may be conscious that he is rather among rivals than friends, but when at home, that restraint is unbecoming. You know the sort of man whose hospitality is repulsive. I dare say you are welcome, but when he shakes hands with you, his hand drops into your hand just like a dead fish. You talk with him, and he is perfectly indifferent. When he is most friendly, there is no freedom in his conversation. Well, now, see the way in which he treats his wife. No love. He is afraid of spoiling her. I recall going to a house where I sat with the husband and I heard a gentle tap at the door, and his lordship said, "Come in." Who should enter but his wife. I soon perceived that she was the principal servant in the house. That was all he accounted her, and she had learned to form no higher estimate of herself. The man had no heart. David did not mean to go through the world in this fashion. A house is all the better for having a heart inside it, and a man is a man and more like God when there is a heart inside his ribs. When he gets home, the children feel that father has a heart, and as they climb his knees and smother him with kisses, they delight to know that he has a warm heart. When he greets his dear relatives and friends, he has a soul that goes beyond his own little self and is enlarged and inspires the whole of the family. Give me heart. That is what David meant when he said he would behave himself wisely. But when he was in his own house, he would walk with a perfect heart. He would be hearty in everything he did and said.

Having noticed those two things—that the heart must be right and the heart must be expressed—the next thing is that the conduct at home must be well regulated. "I will walk within my house with a perfect heart." The Christian at home should be scrupulous in every way within his house. We may have different rooms there, but in whatever room we are, we should seek to walk before God with a perfect heart. Alas, there are many professing believers who fail in this! I have reason to fear that some people who walk as saints abroad behave themselves like devils at home. It is a fact that a *man* is what he is *at home*. This is a simple but a crucial test of character. If a man does not make his family happy and if his example is not that of holiness in the domestic circle, he may make what pretension of godliness he likes, but his religion is worthless. The sooner he gets rid of such a profession, the better for himself, for then he may begin to know what he is and where he is and seek the Lord in spirit and truth. It is at home that the lack of true faith will do most damage. If you are a hypocrite and go into the world, the people who observe you will not be much influenced by your example. They will come to the conclusion that you are what you are, and they will treat you as such, and that will be the end of it. But that will not be so with your little son who sees his father's actions. He is not able to criticize, but he has a wonderful faculty for imitation. And mother, it is not likely that your daughter will begin to say, "Mother is inconsistent." No, she does not know that, but she will take it for granted that mother is right, and her character will be fashioned upon your pattern. As parents you can injure your children for life unless the grace of God prevents it. To our children, especially when they are young, we are, as it were, little gods in our homes. Their conduct is shaped according to the pattern we set before them. Around the kitchen table, if anywhere, holiness should be conspicuous, for there holiness is most beautiful, most useful, and most productive.

It is a blessed thing if we can look back upon a father or mother's example with nothing but unalloyed gratitude to God for both. But there are many who, in looking back, must say, "I thank God I was delivered from the evil influence to which I was subjected as a child." Do not let your child ever have to say that of you, but ask for grace that in your own house you may walk with a perfect heart. For surely, if we are not living in our households as we should, this above all common faults and weaknesses is one of the most disparaging and condemnatory marks with which we can possibly be tainted. In the world we may be under some pressure to live up to a standard, but at home we are left free to be what we really are. Outside, men are checked and kept within decent bounds by the example and the observation of others, so that they are not altogether what they seem, but they are partly regulated by what they wish to appear. Even when they are in the church they are under some restraint. But at home they can think aloud, speak without premeditation, follow their own tastes, and gratify their natural inclinations. At home, therefore, if anywhere, the man is what he is. You need not tell me what appearance you will put on next Sunday morning. I would rather ask you to judge yourself by your lifestyle on Saturday night. How will you be tomorrow morning, and what will you be to your employees, to your children, to your spouse, to your neighbors? If God, by His infinite grace and the power of His Holy Spirit, helps you to walk with a perfect heart at such times and in such places, then will you be an honor to the church of God, and you will have a blessing upon your own soul.

The things that I have written seem to be very homely, but indeed they are most important. I love to expound Christian doctrine: I love to open up the promises. This is all sweet work, but we must have the precepts. We shall never have a large increase to an unholy church, or if we do, that increase will be a curse instead of a blessing. I believe that the greatest power in the world, next to the ministry of the Word, is the holy living of Christian families by the power of the Holy Spirit. Let us plant in this dark world garrisons of holy men and women with their children about them, and this will be a means whereby the world shall be conquered for Christ.

Do pause, think, consider, look; and may God give you grace and sense enough to see that you need wisdom to steer yourself and your family through this voyage of life and that wisdom only is to be had from heaven. May you bend your knee at this very hour and say, "Lord, give me Your grace. Give me a renewed heart. Give me Christ to be my Savior, and help me to behave myself in a perfect way till You shall bring me to see You in heaven in Your glory."

*W*e might gather from our text that this way was
built at great expense, for the making of a road over a long and
rugged country is a costly business. It might be read, "a causeway
shall be there"—it is a way built up by technical skill. Engineering
has done much to tunnel mountains and bridge abysses, but the
greatest triumph of engineering is that which made a way from sin
to holiness, from death to life, from condemnation to perfection.
Who could make a road over the mountains of our iniquities but
Almighty God? None but the God of love would have wished it;
none but the God of wisdom could have devised it; none but the
God of power could have carried it out. It cost the great God the
Jewel of heaven: He emptied out the treasury of His own heart, for
He spared not His own Son but freely delivered Him up for us all.
In the life and death of the Well-beloved, infinite wisdom laid a
firm foundation for the road by which sinners in all ages may
journey home to God. The highway of our God is such a
masterpiece that even those who travel it every day often stand and
wonder and ask how such a way could have been planned and
constructed. Truly that prophecy is fulfilled to the letter: "I will
even make a way in the wilderness, and rivers in the desert. The
beast of the field shall honour me, the dragons and the owls" (Isa.
43:19–20).

Chapter Twelve

The Holy Road

And an highway shall be there, and a way, and it shall be called
The way of holiness; the unclean shall not pass over it; but it shall
be for those: the wayfaring men, though fools, shall not err
therein—Isaiah 35:8.

TWICE HAS ISRAEL come back from captivity. First, when the tribes came out of Egypt and the Lord led them through the wilderness. And the second time, when they returned from captivity in Babylon and the Lord restored them to their land. A third return some us believe still awaits the chosen people. In the day when the grace of God shall change the heart of Israel, the seed of Abraham shall again return into the land that God gave to their fathers by covenant. I think our text looks forward to a future age when the reproach shall be rolled away from Palestine and her deserts shall be made to blossom as the rose. Of these future glories we say but little, for little is known by most of us [this message was given August 1, 1886]. The prophecy is, however, sufficiently clear to make us expect that the Lord will make a way for the return of His ancient people and will restore them to the joy of His salvation. I forbear all theories of prophecy just now, for I feel it more than ever necessary in this evil time to stay close to the beaten road of first principles of the faith. I shall not use the telescope to look into the starry future, but rather use the chart and compass with which to direct our present way. I shall regard the text as having received one fulfillment in the way of salvation by our Lord Jesus Christ. If this is not the literal fulfillment of the prophecy, yet certainly it is its spiritual fulfillment, and for the moment this is the most vital matter to us. Hear it and discern its divine teaching.

The Way to the Heavenly Zion

Zion of old was the place of the one altar of sacrifice and the one mercy seat where the Lord in manifest glory communed with His covenant people. It was to Zion that the tribes went up to offer their national prayer and praise to Jehovah, the God of Israel. Pilgrimage to the holy place was an important part of Israel's religious life. During the invasions of the land, and especially during the captivity, the solemn festivals were neglected, and there seemed to be no way up to the house of God. Then godly men sighed for the tabernacles of God, saying, "When shall I come and appear before God?" (Ps. 42:2). As they could not go there in person, they sent their hearts and their eyes in that direction. Like Daniel, they prayed with their windows open toward Jerusalem (Dan. 6:10). How they longed for a highway by which they could march to Zion! Today I speak of another Jerusalem that is above and of the throne of God the Most High to which we are making our way. Our desire is for the city that has foundations, whose builder and maker is God. Who will bring us there? Who will point out the road?

There Is a Way to God

It is with great joy that we learn from Holy Scripture the great truth set forth in the text: *there is a way to God and heaven.* "And a highway shall be there, and a way." This way from the City of Destruction to the Celestial City is still open and still traveled by companies of pilgrims.

It is noteworthy that this road is both a highway and a way— not two highways or two ways. Many roads lead to ruin, but only one road leads to salvation. So many men, so many minds; but if we are men of God, all our minds are one as to the one way that leads to God. We trust in the same Savior and are made alive by the same Spirit, and as a consequence, our experience has a vital unity in it. The scenes and circumstances of our lives differ widely, but the joys and sorrows, the struggles and the victories are the same, and one hope fills our hearts. There is a unity of the divine way, truth, and life in believers' lives. We differ in the pace with which we travel the way, but the way itself is one: Christ is all and in all. Let us not be deceived about it: there are not two roads to heaven. If anyone tells you that there are two gospels, you may remind them of Paul's words: "another gospel: which is not another; but there be some that trouble you, and would pervert the gospel of Christ" (Gal. 1:6–7).

What that "way" is we learn from John 14:6: "Jesus saith unto him, I am the way, the truth, and the life: no man cometh unto the Father, but by me." Believing in Jesus, we enter upon the way; receiving His Spirit into our hearts, we stand in the way; following our Redeemer's footsteps, we walk in the way; and holding fast to His leadership, we reach the end of the way. When we find Jesus, we find the way of truth, the way of life, the way of peace, the way of holiness. He is not only the way but also the end to all those who put their trust in Him. There is but one Christ, and therefore but one way of salvation. He is the same yesterday, today, and forever; and those who pretend that He changes with the centuries talk as idle dreamers, knowing nothing of the matter. God has given us a way to Himself in the person of His Son Jesus Christ. Why should He give us another? What other can there be?

This way, you will note, is made through the wilderness: "a highway shall be *there*"—through the deserts, where the sand is always shifting, where if the traveler once loses his bearings he is doomed to certain death. A way is made for us through the deserts of sin and the wildernesses of sorrow, over hills of doubt and mountains of fear. That way runs close at your feet, poor wanderer, even though you may now be lost amid the habitation of the dragons of despair. The King's highway is made through the wilderness: every valley is exalted, and every mountain and hill is laid low. Oh, you who are so faint that you lie down to die in despair, lift up your eyes and see the door of hope. You think it not possible that there can be an open road for you to travel on to God, but there is such a road, for our text clearly states, "a highway shall be there." I am comforted that although many have wandered deeply into error, vice, and hardness of heart or into the gloomy valley of despondency, even there this highway runs in a straight line. God, who makes rivers in high places and fountains in the midst of deserts, has built up a royal road by which the Lord's banished may return to Himself. From death's dark door up to heaven's pearly gate the line is unbroken, for Jesus Christ our Savior has borne our death and brought us life and immortality.

We might gather from our text that this way was built at great expense, for the making of a road over a long and rugged country is a costly business. It might be read, "a causeway shall be there"—it is a way built up by technical skill. Engineering has done much to tunnel mountains and bridge abysses, but the greatest triumph of engineering is that which made a way from sin to holiness, from death to life, from condemnation to perfection. Who could make a road over the mountains of our iniquities but Almighty God? None but the God of love would have wished it; none but the God of wisdom could have devised it; none but the God of power could have carried it out. It cost the great God the Jewel of heaven: He emptied out the treasury of His own heart, for He spared not His own Son but freely delivered Him up for us all. In the life and death of the Well-beloved, infinite wisdom laid a firm foundation for the road by which sinners in all ages may journey home to God. The highway of our God is such a masterpiece that even those who travel it every day often stand and wonder and ask how such a way could have been planned and constructed. Truly that prophecy is fulfilled to the letter: "I will even make a way in the wilderness, and rivers in the desert. The beast of the field shall honour me, the dragons and the owls" (Isa. 43:19–20).

This road has lasted now these thousands of years. It is still in good traveling condition and will never be closed until all the chosen wayfarers shall have reached the many mansions of the Father's house. Conspicuous to all beholders, the everlasting causeway remains unbroken and unaltered, and fresh caravans of pilgrims continually traverse it.

This way, being made by divine power, is appointed by divine authority to be the King's highway. Whoever travels by this road is under the protection of the King of kings. Be sure it leads to the right end and runs in the best direction, for the Lord never made an error and never failed in what He attempted. This is no roundabout way, or broken route, or blind alley. Let your faith abide in it, and it shall receive its reward. When I preach Jesus Christ as the way of life, I always feel that I take no responsibility upon myself at all. I am only publishing a proclamation for which the King Himself is responsible. We deliver a royal message when we teach the doctrine of the sacrifice of Jesus Christ, for it is He "Whom God hath set forth to be a propitiation through faith in his blood" (Rom. 3:25). When we tell of the way of salvation by faith in Jesus Christ, we are not planning a track or making a road but simply are pointing to one that has long been used. If it were a highway of our own making you might criticize it, but in that it is a way of God's making, you are commanded to walk in it. To quit this road for another is to despise the wisdom and grace of God in Christ Jesus, preferring the idle inventions of men. This cannot lead to any good, either in this life or in the next.

This highway has conducted many already to God. It is said to be "a highway" and "a way." It is not only a highway by design but also a way by use and traffic. It is trodden hard by ten thousand times ten thousand feet that have joyfully and safely traversed it from end to end. Behold the cloud of witnesses in glory who will all tell you that Jesus was their way to victory, their one and only way to life eternal. Thousands of us are still on the road, and we can speak well of it; yes, we can sing in the ways of the Lord. Though we at times faint in the way, we find no fault with the road. "Her ways are ways of pleasantness, and all her paths are peace" (Prov. 3:17). It is our joy and our delight to walk where our Savior led the way and where apostles and prophets are our fellow travelers. We delight to look forward to its end: how glorious the prospect! But we are not ashamed to look back and admire the path of grace in the years that are past. We glory in the fact that we are on our way to God and shall soon behold Him whom not having seen we love and in whom believing we even now rejoice with joy unspeakable and full of glory (1 Pet. 1:8).

Yes, there is a way to heaven. Let the glad tidings be reported everywhere: there is a way to God. Let no one say, "I cannot possibly reach a home with God in heaven." Wherever you may be, "a highway shall be there"; wherever you now are, a way is made by which you may at once proceed to reconciliation, peace, purity, salvation. Oh, that you may at once ask the way to Zion!

The Name of the Way

Our text also tells us the name of this way: "it shall be called the Way of holiness." The way to God by Jesus Christ is the *Via Sacra,* the Holy Road. The way of faith is not contrary to holiness, it is the way of holiness. There is no way to heaven but by holiness. We have a great need to insist upon this in these days, for together with laxity of thought and dubiousness of doctrinal teaching, there has come into vogue a great looseness of morals. I am not speaking now to the outside world, but I dread this declension in the church. Professing Christians are becoming less and less strict as to their pleasures. We hear of Christian ministers doing that which those who formerly occupied their pulpits never dreamed of doing themselves. Everywhere I see professing Christians doing what their ancestors would have viewed with holy indignation.

The way to heaven—if it is anything—is a way of holiness. If the way we follow is not a holy way and a separated way, it is not God's way. If we do not follow the way of distinction from the world, we are not following Christ. He who is not holy on the way will not come to that holy end where the holy God reveals Himself in His glory. If you are ever in doubt about which is the right path, remember these words of the Savior: "Strait is the gate, and narrow is the way, which leadeth unto life, and few there be that find it" (Matt. 7:14). Prefer strictness to laxity. Do not mistake me, for I wish to be understood even if I am charged with censoriousness. We need to pull up every now and then and ask ourselves, "Which out of these two courses is the right way?" In these times exceedingly clever people are declaring new roads and extolling them in this fashion: "Here you have a road worthy of the road for the cultured and advanced." Your Savior lifts His warning hand as He cries, "Broad is the way, that leadeth to destruction, and many there be that go in thereat" (Matt. 7:13). Even if you are charged with legalism, still select that way that the saints of old have chosen, perhaps unpleasing to the flesh, but pleasing to God—the strait and narrow road that leads to life eternal.

God's way is the way of holiness, for He has founded it upon holy truth. God is not unholy in the saving of any sinner. No sinner is saved without justice being executed to the full in the full expiation of the Lord Jesus Christ. Eternal principles forbade a righteous God to wink at sin, and He has not done so. Justice is absolutely vindicated by the redemption of Christ.

Those who follow that road do so by a holy trust. If we would be saved, we must have a holy faith in a holy Savior, from whom we look for holy blessings. We must not believe that Christ will save us *in* our sins—that would be unholy faith. We must look to Him to save us *from* our sins, for that is holy faith. We must trust that He will cast the evil out of us and that He will purify us to Himself, to be a people zealous of good works. We preach no faith without works, for that is a dead faith. Although we speak the word *grace* without hesitation, we also assert that the grace that does not lead to holiness is not the grace of God at all, nor do they who receive it prove themselves to be God's elect.

God's way is also the way of holy living. The man who believes in Jesus Christ will be found purging himself from the ways of sinners. He will be holy, harmless, undefiled, and separate from sinners. He will pant and aspire after perfect holiness, and if he does not immediately attain it, he will still groan toward it, still longing to be made like Christ. The way to heaven not only is a holy way but also, according to the text, is to be called so by those who speak of it. The way that God has marked out for His people to follow is a conspicuously holy and Godlike way. Let us keep to it.

A Select Way

Further dwelling on our text, *this way is a select way.* It is written, "The unclean shall not pass over it; but it shall be for those." The unclean are excluded. They were excluded from the house of the Lord, and here they are excluded from the sacred way of Israel. Spiritually, this means that unless we are washed in the blood of Christ and renewed in the spirit of our minds by the Holy Spirit, we are not in the way of God. To be unclean does not exclude you from the possibility of salvation, for there are ways by which the unclean can be made pure. You cannot enter in this way of life except by being cleansed by the atonement and renewed by the

Holy Spirit. By the way of forgiveness you can pass into this way, for the Lord waits to be gracious to you and to wash you clean. Pardon and regeneration are freely given to all who desire them, and you must have both or you cannot tread the sacred way.

It is a select way, for it is reserved for a select people: "it shall be for those." "Those"—who are they? You need to look back from the text and you will read of some who made the wilderness and the solitary place to be glad. You read of some whose blind eyes were opened, some whose deaf ears were unstopped. You read of lame men who were made to leap as a hart and of dumb men who began to sing. This highway is reserved for those upon whom a miracle of grace has been performed, for those on whom the Messiah has laid His healing hand, for those who love and delight in holy things. Though often of a fearful heart, they are bold to hold on in the sacred way, and they shall never be driven from it. The pure in heart shall see God (Matt. 5:8) and travel the way to God: "it shall be for those."

Especially at the end of our text we read that this way is for the ransomed: "the redeemed shall walk there." If you believe in Jesus Christ, you have been redeemed with His precious blood and the way of grace is yours. Do you look only to Him who poured out His soul to death on your behalf? If so, you are in the way, and you may walk there without any fear of ever being driven out. He that once comes into this way, Christ will never cast him out, and He is the Lord of the way. You shall walk there until you shall see His face with joy. This way, though open to all who come with willing hearts, is a select way that no unrepentant soul can walk in.

Another fact makes it very select. God shall be with those who walk this road. This way of holiness is a way in which God walks with His people, revealing Himself to them, drawing them nearer to Himself, and keeping them in happy union with Himself. It is a blessed thing to think of heaven at the end, but it is an equally blessed thing to think of God with us on the way. We too seldom consider the blessedness of the way to heaven. Even to be on the way there is a marvel of grace. Such stores of covenant blessings are provided and distributed along the way that even as pilgrims we are a blessed people. The presence of God with us on our journey is our choicest joy. If, after all, there should be no heaven, my present life has been rendered happy by walking in the way of faith and obedience to God. Godliness has the promise of the life that is now, and that promise never fails. We have such joy and peace in walking with God that we can bear witness that in keeping God's commandments there is great reward.

A Plain Way

I must pass on to notice one more matter about this way: *the way that God has appointed is a plain way.* We are bound to be thankful for a way that is suitable for ordinary people. You would think from some people's talk that faith is a difficult thing, only to be understood by the cultured few. You must be a scientist or a scholarly critic before you can understand the modern gospel. It is not so with the gospel of Jesus. Oftentimes, highly educated people miss this way altogether, while simple people perceive it and walk in it. Simple truth is needful for dying men and women. The gospel that suits little children is that which saves souls; the gospel of the common people is the only gospel. The most educated must find their wisdom in the cross—or die a fool. In times of trial, men are not helped by speculations, mystifications, and refinings; they need sure and plain truth to build their hopes upon. The taste of our present time is all for that which is novel, original, and pretendedly profound. Give me the daily bread such as Jesus divided among the men and women and children, and I will leave the stones of philosophy to those who care to try their teeth on them. The most plain truth is the best.

The gospel of God needs no wisdom of words to commend it, and therefore the Apostle Paul says, "We use great plainness of speech" (2 Cor. 3:12). The true gospel is as plain as a wooden post. What does the text say? "Wayfaring men, though fools, shall not err therein." No one will err about the way to God if he really resolves to follow that way. The Spirit of God will guide those whose hearts are set upon coming to God. It is the wayfaring man who does not err. Critics will be sure to err, but the true pilgrim, the wayfaring man who is actually travelling, shall not err. If you want to go to heaven, the way is laid down in the Scriptures so plainly that little children may find it. But if you only want to talk about the road and about the difficulties of travellers in it, then the way is difficult indeed. If you choose to puzzle yourselves about

His gospel, God will give you over to be puzzled. He who must be wiser than God shall end in being more brutish than any man. If you wish to find the way to heaven, there it is: "Behold the Lamb of God." Believe in Jesus and be saved. That Jesus is the way to peace and holiness is as plain in Scripture as the nose on your face. What more teaching do you want? What more assurance do you require? If your heart is inclined to see, there is light enough, and the cross is clear enough: look and live. Those who desire to see shall see, but those who shut their eyes only prove the truth of the old proverb, "There are none so blind as those who do not wish to see." He who says, "I will arise and go to my Father," shall not miss the way. He who has received the desire from the Lord shall by the Lord perceive the way. "The wayfaring man shall not err."

That wayfaring man may be a great fool in other matters, but he shall be no fool upon this matter. He may be ignorant about science, politics, and business, but if the Lord has made him willing to be a wayfaring man with his face to Zion, he shall not mistake in his journey along the holy way. God will instruct him in the vital points The main thing is to know the most necessary truth and practice it. Our Lord said, "But one thing is needful" (Luke 10:42). The chief thing is to know how sin is pardoned, how a sinner is justified and sanctified. There are a thousand things that a man may not know, and he may not be much the worse for not knowing them; but to not know the Lord Jesus is to be ignorant of the path of life. If a man knows the Lord Christ, he knows the way to eternal happiness. Let every man gain all the instruction he can, but let him not think that mere knowledge will be of great value to him in heavenly things, for the tree of knowledge of good and evil brought no good to our race. I often have wished that I could forget many things that I once thought necessary to know! I would resolve with Paul to know nothing among you save Jesus Christ and Him crucified (1 Cor. 2:2). There, let the bubble burst and the scum be blown away. Let that fire consume the glitter and tinsel. What are they when weighed with one ingot of the real gold of the knowledge of Him who loved us and gave Himself for us? Let us choose the right way. Let us look up to God and say, "Thou wilt shew me the path of life" (Ps. 16:11).

A Safe Way

   The last word of our text teaches us that it is a safe way. "No lion shall be there." Plenty of lions prowl up and down the side of the road, but they cannot "go up thereon." He who keeps to the center of the road, though he may hear the lion roar, shall not meet it in the way. No ravenous beasts shall be found there, for the way is not to their liking. Tropical animals cannot live in northern climates, nor lions in the holy way. There is one lion that those who make Jesus their way need never be afraid of: that is the lion of unpardoned sin. If you believe in Jesus Christ, your iniquities are forgiven you for His name's sake. Another lion also roars upon us but cannot devour us, namely, temptation: you shall not be tempted above what you are able to bear (1 Cor. 10:13). We read of some who followed their own way, that the Lord sent lions among them (2 Kings 17:25), but He drives away the lions from those who keep the right way. Lions are afraid of fire, and the Lord is a wall of fire round about His people. As for that grim lion of death of which some speak, it does not exist. Death to a believer is rather an angel than a lion. The valley through which we are to pass is the valley not of death but of the shadow of death. For the believer there is no substance in death; it is only a shadow. The shadow of a dog cannot bite, the shadow of a sword cannot wound, and the shadow of death cannot destroy. Go on without fearing any evil, for the Lord is with you; His rod and His staff are your comfort (Ps. 23:4). No ravenous beast can harm you, for it is written, "There shall no evil befall thee" (Ps. 91:10). Walk with God, and "thou shalt tread upon the lion and adder: the young lion and the dragon shalt thou trample under feet" (Ps. 91:13). To be safe we must be holy. To be holy we must trust in Christ Jesus the Lord.

Our Response to This Holy Way

   The first thing is *to carefully discriminate* between the roads before us. Beware of false prophets. "Believe not every spirit, but try the spirits whether they are of God" (1 John 4:1). When you see a road that looks broad, smooth, pleasant, and well-bordered with flowers, say to yourself, "There are many ways, but since only one leads to eternal life, I must be careful. Is this the way of holiness? If it is not the holy way, it is not the road I dare follow." Do not believe that sincerity is enough; you need truth as well. If you sincerely mistake the road and go the wrong direction, you will never get to your destination. If you sincerely drink poison, it will kill you. If you sincerely believe a lie, you will suffer the consequences. You must not only be sincere but also be right. Therefore, submit your judgment to the Word of the Lord. This infallible Book is given to you, and the infallible Spirit waits to instruct you as to its meaning. Cry unto the Wise One for wisdom. Yield your minds to the teaching of Him who is the way, the truth, and the life, so you shall not be deceived, but you shall walk in holiness.

The next thing is that when you know the road, you should *scrupulously keep in it*, for many ways branch from it. Let no one draw you aside from it. It is one straight line. Keep to it, even as the stars keep in their courses. Gird up the loins of your mind with the truth. May the Holy Spirit so rest upon you that you may have no desire to leave the strait and narrow way, no desire to step aside from it, even for a moment. He that endures to the end, the same shall be saved (Matt. 10:22). Those who run well with the faith but then are hindered, what shall become of them? Why this: that it were better for them not to have known the way of righteousness than to turn from it after they have known it. To the end! Hold on and hold out, or your faith will prove to be a thing of no account.

Are we in the holy way? Then let us *be very earnest in telling other people of it*. The other day a traveller on a country road wished to know the way to a certain spot. He inquired of one who sat by the roadside, but the only answer he got was a vacant stare and a shake of the head. A little later he found that the poor man was a deaf mute. I am afraid there are many such Christians nowadays: they are spiritually deaf to the woes of others and silent as to giving them either instruction or encouragement. All they seem to do is to shake their wise heads, as if they knew a great deal more than they meant to tell. Why do you not tell others the way to heaven? Why do you not hear the cry that is going up to God everywhere for spiritual instruction? How is it that so many Christians are content to occupy their pews but never go forth to declare what they have found in Jesus? I fear some professing believers cannot tell the way because they do not know it. You cannot tell what you don't know. God grant that we may never stretch the arm of our testimony beyond the sleeve of our experience! It shall be well for any minister if it may be written upon his tombstone, "He never preached what he did not practice." May you Christian workers so live what you teach that you may teach what you live!

It is a horrible thing to stand like a signpost to point to the road, but never to run in that road yourself. It would be well if we were always ready to tell the way to heaven to everybody, whether they want to know it or not. Possibly the men we are most likely to bless are those who at this present moment do not desire to know the gospel. If we point out the way to them, God may ordain that our describing the path will be an effectual influence for leading them into it. There are two occasions in which we should point out the way to all around, namely, "in season, and out of season" (2 Tim. 4:2). We shall be clear of the blood of men if we show them the way, entreating them to walk in it. If we do not do this, they may perish for lack of knowing the road, and their blood may then be required at our hands.

Finally, what should we do in connection with this? I would say, if you are not in the road, may the Lord help you to *get into it immediately*. "What is to be done to reach the heavenly city?" asks one. A notable divine once gave this direction: "The way to heaven is, turn to the right and keep straight on." I would add, turn when you come to the cross; only one turn is needed, but that must be a thorough turn, and one in which you persevere. Keep straight on till you come to glory. Trust in the Lord Jesus Christ, and you have eternal life.

"But," says one, "I have begun to trust Christ, but I am always afraid of myself lest I should go back after all." This is by no means an unhealthy fear when you consider the matter in reference to your own strength, but there is another light in which to regard it. Trust in the Lord for final perseverance, and He will give it to you. One thing I would earnestly recommend to you who are afraid of backsliding and apostasy: say to yourself, "Whether I get to Canaan or not, I will never go back to Egypt. I will die with my face toward God and holiness." The soul that can keep this solemn resolve to never return to the country from where he has been redeemed will surely reach the promised rest. Your carcass will not fall in the wilderness if your face is toward the Lord Jesus, His promise, and His throne. No, never will we love this evil world nor bow before its idols. We have lifted our hand to the Lord, and we cannot go back. If God has brought you only a little out of your sins, I pray that you may press forward.

"Lord God, if I am cast away, if You never give me joy again, yet I will never cease to look to Your mercy in Christ Jesus, for there only have I hope. By Your grace I will die with my face to the cross." Did you ever hear of anybody who perished in that position? No. It shall never be reported in heaven above or in hell beneath that a soul died in the way—Christ being that way. No soul can perish whose eyes look toward the five wounds of Jesus crucified. He is the way, the living way, the only way, the sure way: follow Him. Do as the blind man did who followed Jesus in the way: rise up now, for He calls you. Look to Jesus! Take this road of refuge, this way of grace. May God the Holy Spirit help you to take to the way at once, without delay! Unto you shall be salvation, and unto the Lord of the way shall be glory forever and ever.